Spiralize now!

80 DELICIOUS, HEALTHY RECIPES FOR YOUR SPIRALIZER

DENISE SMART

hamlyn

An Hachette UK Company
www.hachette.co.uk

First published in Great Britain in 2015 by Hamlyn,
a division of
Octopus Publishing Group Ltd
Carmelite House
50 Victoria Embankment
London EC4Y 0DZ
www.octopusbooks.co.uk

ISBN 978-0-600-63272-6

A CIP catalogue record for this book is available from the British Library

Printed and bound in China

10 9 8 7 6 5 4 3 2

Both imperial and metric measurements have been given in all recipes. Use one set of measurements only and not a mixture of both.

Standard level spoon measurement are used in all recipes.
1 tablespoon = one 15 ml spoon
1 teaspoon = one 5 ml spoon

Eggs should be medium, milk should be full fat and fresh herbs should be used unless otherwise stated.

contents

it's time to get spiralizing 4

light bites 8

salads 32

mains 50

sides and extras 84

sweet treats 104

index 126

acknowledgements 128

it's time to get spiralizing

The benefits of spiralizing

A spiralizer is an affordable, easy-to-use cutting machine with a selection of blades that you can use to create a variety of different noodles and ribbons from vegetables and fruit. It's the ideal gadget for health-conscious cooks as it can help you to cut back on refined carbohydrates, such as pasta and rice, by replacing them with spiralized fruit and vegetables so that you can enjoy your meals while eating fewer calories. A spiralizer will also encourage you to include more fruit and vegetables in your diet and can be a life-saver for those following special diets, such as low-carb, gluten-free and raw food.

Spiralizing can help you to save time as it's really quick and easy to prepare fruit and vegetables using a spiralizer. And spiralizing can also reduce cooking times because many of the vegetables and fruit prepared in this way can be eaten raw or just cooked very lightly, which also means that all nutrients are retained.

Choosing a spiralizer

There are many brands on the market, but all essentially work in the same way. The larger horizontal and vertical ones are better for heavier root vegetables and everyday use, but small hand-held ones are ideal if you are cooking for one or for occasional use or for creating garnishes.

Spiralizers usually come with several different blades, each of which creates a different shape. For this book, I used a horizontal spiralizer with three blades, which I have called the 3 mm (1/8 inch) spaghetti blade, the 6 mm (1/4 inch) flat noodle blade and the ribbon blade.

How to use a horizontal spiralizer

1 Attach the machine to the worktop using the suction feet or lever.

2 Insert the blade you wish to use into the machine.

3 Prepare the fruit or vegetable according to the recipe: peel it, if required, trim off the ends to make a flat surface and cut in half widthways, if necessary.

4 Attach one end of the prepared fruit or vegetable to the blade and then clamp the other end of the vegetable to the spiky grip on the crank handle.

5 Grasp the side handle for leverage, turn the crank handle and apply a little pressure so that the fruit or vegetable is pressed between the blade and the handle – this will create spirals.

6 Finally, remove the long core and a round disc that remains at the end of the spiralizing process.

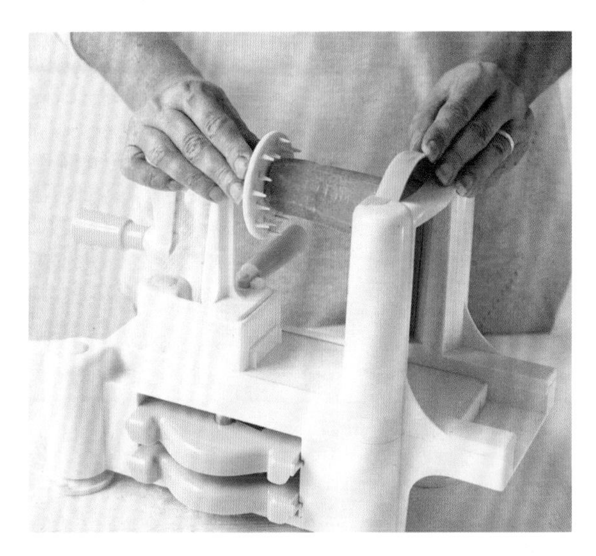

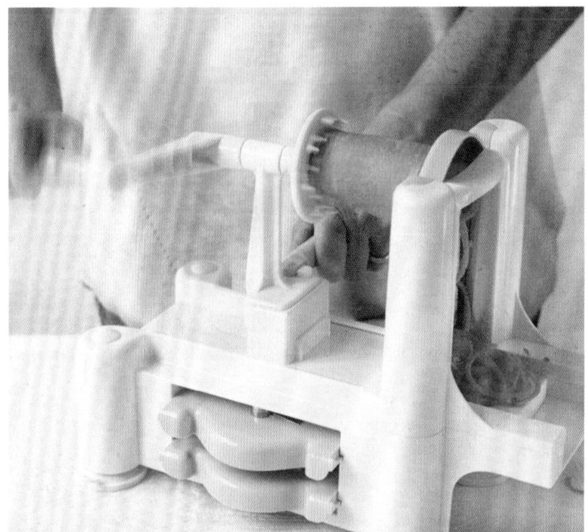

Tips for successful spiralizing

- Choose firm fruit and vegetables without stones, seeds or hollow centres: the only exceptions are butternut squash (just use the non-bulbous end) and green papaya.

- Vegetables and fruit should not be soft or juicy – pineapples, melons and aubergines will fall apart when you spiralize them.

- Choose vegetables that are as straight as possible. Occasionally you may have to re-centre the vegetables to avoid half moon shapes.

- Make sure the ends of fruit and vegetables are as flat as possible by slicing a small piece off either end. Uneven ends can make it difficult to secure the fruit or vegetable to the spiralizer and may cause them dislodge or misalign.

- If you find that a fruit or vegetable is not spiralizing very well, it may be because there is not a large enough surface area for the spiralizer to grip to. For best results, lengths should be no longer than 12 cm (5 inches) and about 3.5 cm (1½ inches) in diameter. Cut any large vegetables in half widthways.

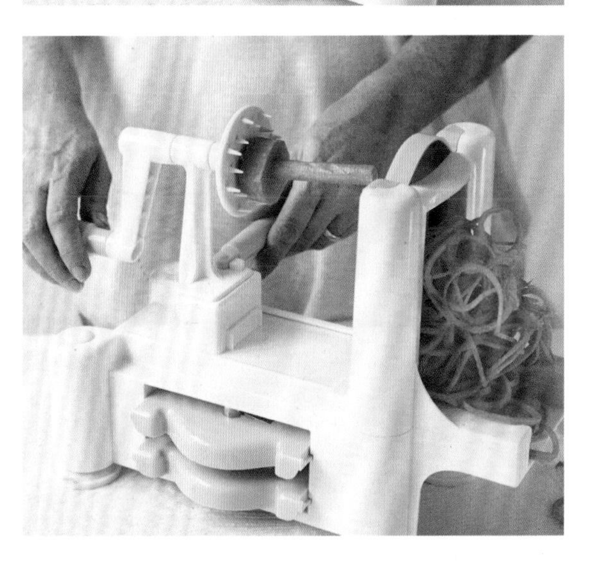

- You will be left with a long core and a round disc at the end of the spiralizing process. Save these cores to use when making soups or for snacks.

- A lot of juice is squeezed out of fruit and vegetables when you spiralize them, especially from courgettes, carrots, cucumber, potatoes, apples and pears. Just pat the spirals dry on kitchen paper before use.

- Be careful when cleaning your spiralizer as the blades are very sharp. Wash the machine in hot soapy water and use a small kitchen brush or toothbrush to remove stubborn bits of fruit or vegetables from the blades.

Which fruit and vegetables can be spiralized?
I tested many different types of fruit and vegetables while writing and testing the recipes for this book. To save you wasting precious fruit and vegetables, here is a list of the ones that I found to work best.

Apples There's no need to peel or core apples, just trim the ends and spiralize whole – the core is left behind in the machine. Spiralized apples are perfect for use in salads and savoury dishes as well as desserts. Remember that the spiralized apple will turn brown very quickly so use immediately or dress with lemon juice.

Beetroot There's no need to peel fresh beetroot, just wash the skin, flatten the ends and spiralize whole. Eat raw in salads or bake into delicious beetroot crisps.

Broccoli Don't throw away broccoli stems when you cook broccoli – the stems spiralizes really well. For best results, stir-fry or steam the spiralized broccoli stems.

Butternut squash To avoid the seeds, you should only use the non-bulbous end of the squash. Snip any really long strands of spiralized squash into smaller pieces using scissors – this will make the squash easier to eat.

Carrots Choose large carrots for spiralizing. Eat spiralized carrots raw in salads or steam carrot ribbons to create a delicious accompaniment.

Celeriac The best way to prepare this root vegetable is to use a sharp knife to remove the knobbly bits from the celeriac and then peel it, cut it in half widthways and trim to make the ends flat. Spiralized celeriac works well in gratins, soups and remoulade.

Courgettes Forget about regular pasta, spiralized courgettes make perfect 'courgetti' (courgette spaghetti). They can be eaten raw or very lightly steamed, boiled or stir-fried.

Cucumbers Once you've spiralized the cucumber you just need to pat the spirals or ribbons dry. Cucumbers make beautiful ribbons for use in salads.

Daikon radish or mooli Spiralized daikon radish and mooli make a great alternative to rice noodles.

Green papaya You can find green papaya in Asian supermarkets. Although it is hollow it attaches to the spiralizer well. Perfect eaten raw in salads.

Green plantains Choose plantains that are as straight as possible and remove the tough outer green skin. Spiralized green plantain is delicious in curries.

Jerusalem artichokes Choose large artichokes. There's no need to peel these knobbly vegetables, all you need to do is wash them. If you're not using the spiralized artichokes immediately, place them in a bowl of water with a little lemon juice to prevent them discolouring.

Onions Onions can be spiralized whole – all you need to do is trim the ends before you start. You can use spiralized onions to replace chopped ones in recipes or turn them into onion bhajis or crispy onion spirals.

Parsnips Choose large fat parsnips for best results. Add them to a rosti or make parsnip crisps.

Pears Choose firm pears for spiralizing as pears that are too ripe will add too much moisture to some of the dessert recipes. To prepare the pears for spiralizing, just trim down the pointy ends.

Potatoes and sweet potatoes Prepare potatoes by either scrubbing or peeling and then trim the ends and cut in half widthways if very large. Sweet potatoes are great for adding colour to a dish.

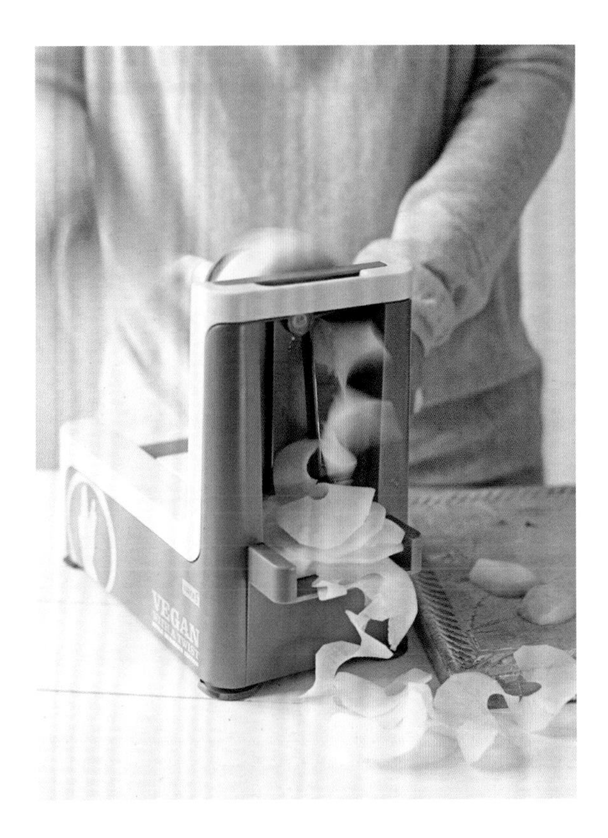

Swedes Peel off the outside skin and cut into large chunks with flat ends to attach to the spiralizer. Use in rostis or fritters or mixed with potatoes as a topping.

Cooking and storing spiralized vegetables

Spiralized vegetables can be eaten raw or cooked very quickly. The best cooking methods for spiralized vegetables are steaming, stir-frying and simmering in boiling water. You can also bake and roast spiralized vegetables such as potatoes, parsnips, beetroot and butternut squash in half the time you would cook large chunks of the same vegetables. It is very easy to overcook vegetable 'spaghetti', so keep a close eye on it while cooking to make sure it doesn't fall apart.

Most spiralized vegetables can be stored in an airtight container in the refrigerator for up to 4 days, so you can prepare your vegetables in advance or spiralize extra and save the rest for another day. The exceptions are spiralized cucumber, which will only keep for about 2 days because of its high water content, and apples, pears and potatoes, which quickly oxidize and turn brown and so are best prepared as needed.

light bites

vegetable noodle miso soup

Serves 4
Prepare in 5 minutes
Cook in 10 minutes

900 ml (1½ pints) hot vegetable stock
2 tablespoons white miso paste
2 teaspoons grated fresh root ginger
2 carrots, peeled, ends trimmed and halved widthways
2 courgettes, ends trimmed and halved widthways
150 g (5 oz) fresh or frozen edamame beans
2 tablespoons chopped fresh coriander

Place the vegetable stock, miso paste and ginger in a saucepan. Bring to the boil, then reduce the heat and simmer for 3–4 minutes.

Meanwhile, using a spiralizer fitted with a 3 mm (⅛ inch) spaghetti blade, spiralize the carrots and courgettes.

Add the spiralized carrots and courgettes and the edamame beans to the soup and simmer for 3–4 minutes, until just tender. Stir in the coriander and serve immediately.

prawn rice paper wraps

Serves 2
Prepare in 10 minutes

10 cm (4 inch) piece mooli, peeled and ends trimmed
½ carrot, peeled and ends trimmed
1 spring onion, finely sliced
25 g (1 oz) bean sprouts
4 tablespoons chopped fresh coriander
125 g (4 oz) cooked peeled prawns
4 dried rice paper wrappers (banh trang), about 20.5 cm (8 inches) in diameter (available from Asian supermarkets)
1 tablespoon fish sauce
8 mint leaves
sweet chilli dipping sauce, to serve

Using a spiralizer fitted with a 3 mm (⅛ inch) spaghetti blade, spiralize the mooli and carrot.

Place the spiralized vegetables in a bowl with the spring onion, bean sprouts, coriander and prawns and mix well.

One at a time, place each rice paper wrapper in a bowl of warm water for about 30 seconds, until the wrapper softens and turns opaque, and then remove, shake off any excess water and place on a board. Brush the middle of the wrapper with a little fish sauce, add 2 mint leaves and then arrange a little of the prawn and vegetable mixture along the centre. Fold over both ends of the wrap and then roll up and cover with a damp cloth. Repeat with the remaining wrappers and filling.

Cut each roll in half and serve immediately with the dipping sauce.

courgette, feta and mint fritters

Serves 4
Prepare in 10 minutes
Cook in 15 minutes

3 courgettes, ends trimmed and cut in half widthways
4 spring onions, chopped
4 tablespoons chopped mint
125 g (4 oz) self-raising flour
1 teaspoon ground cumin
2 eggs, lightly beaten
125 g (4 oz) feta cheese, crumbled
1 tablespoon olive oil, for frying
salt and freshly ground black pepper
tomato salsa, to serve

Using a spiralizer fitted with a 3 mm (⅛ inch) spaghetti blade, spiralize the courgettes.

In a large bowl, mix together the spiralized courgettes, spring onions, mint, flour and cumin. Stir in the eggs, mix well and season with salt and pepper. Gently fold in the feta.

Heat a little oil in a large frying pan over a medium heat. Cooking 4 fritters at a time, add heaped tablespoons of the batter to the pan, flatten slightly and cook for 3 minutes on each side, until golden. Repeat until all the batter is used up. Serve the fritters with a spoonful of tomato salsa.

Mexican baked potato nests

Serves 4
Prepare in 10 minutes
Cook in 20 minutes

- 2 potatoes, about 375 g (12 oz), peeled and ends trimmed
- 1 small onion, ends trimmed
- 2 tablespoons olive oil
- 75 g (3 oz) chorizo, diced
- 1 garlic clove, crushed
- 1 mild green chilli, deseeded and finely chopped
- ½ small yellow pepper, cored, deseeded and diced
- 1 x 200 g (7 oz) can chopped tomatoes
- 1 teaspoon tomato ketchup
- 1 tablespoon chopped fresh coriander
- 4 eggs
- smoked paprika, for sprinkling
- salt and freshly ground black pepper

This recipe, a play on the popular Mexican dish huevos rancheros, is perfect served for breakfast or as a light meal.

Using a spiralizer fitted with a 3 mm (⅛ inch) spaghetti blade, spiralize the potatoes and onion, keeping them separate.

Place the spiralized potatoes in a large bowl, add the oil, season with salt and pepper and then use your hands to toss the potatoes to coat them in the oil and seasoning. Divide the potatoes between 4 Yorkshire pudding tins, each about 10 cm (4 inches) in diameter. Bake the potato nests in a preheated oven, 180°C (350°F), Gas Mark 4, for 10 minutes.

Meanwhile, place the chorizo in a frying pan and cook over a medium heat for 2–3 minutes, until the oil has been released from the chorizo. Stir in the spiralized onion, garlic, chilli and yellow pepper and cook over a moderate heat, stirring frequently, for about 2–3 minutes, until the pepper is soft. Stir in the tomatoes and ketchup and season with salt and pepper. Bring to the boil, then reduce the heat and simmer for 2–3 minutes, until the mixture has thickened. Stir in the coriander and season to taste.

Remove the potato nests from the oven and use the back of a spoon to press down the centre of each nest to make a hollow. Divide the tomato mixture between the nests and then use the back of a spoon to make 4 shallow dips.

Break an egg into each shallow dip (don't worry if the egg runs out slightly). Return to the oven and bake for a further 6–7 minutes, until the eggs are just set. Sprinkle over a little smoked paprika and serve immediately.

mooli, carrot and cucumber laksa

Serves 4
Prepare in 5 minutes
Cook in 10 minutes

500 g (1 lb) mooli, peeled, ends trimmed and halved widthways
1 large carrot, peeled, ends trimmed and halved widthways
¼ cucumber, ends trimmed
6 tablespoons laksa paste
150 g (5 oz) green beans, trimmed and halved
1 x 400 ml (13 fl oz) can reduced-fat coconut milk
750 ml (1¼ pints) hot vegetable stock
1 tablespoon palm or soft brown sugar
125 g (4 oz) bean sprouts
1 x 225 g (7½ oz) can bamboo shoots, drained
2 tablespoons chopped fresh coriander
4 spring onions, chopped
1 red chilli, finely sliced
4 lime wedges, to serve

Flat rice noodles are replaced with spiralized mooli in this spicy soup recipe. You could add some cooked prawns to the dish if you like, stirring them in at the end of the cooking time to heat through.

Using a spiralizer fitted with a 6 mm (¼ inch) flat noodle blade, spiralize the mooli. Change to a 3 mm (⅛ inch) spaghetti blade and spiralize the carrot and cucumber, keeping the mooli, carrot and cucumber separate.

Place the laksa paste, spiralized mooli and beans in a large saucepan and stir to coat the vegetables in the paste. Cook over a medium heat for 1–2 minutes, then stir in the coconut milk, stock and sugar and simmer for 2 minutes. Add the spiralized carrot, bean sprouts and bamboo shoots and simmer for 3 minutes, until all the vegetables are just tender. Stir in the coriander.

Divide the soup between 4 bowls and top with the spring onions, chilli and spiralized cucumber. Serve immediately, with wedges of lime to squeeze over.

courgette and haloumi bruschetta

Serves 2
Prepare in 5 minutes
Cook in 5–10 minutes

1 large courgette, ends trimmed and halved widthways
1 tablespoon olive oil
1 teaspoon thyme leaves
1 garlic clove, crushed
4 slices haloumi
4 slices ciabatta, toasted
salt and freshly ground black pepper

Using a spiralizer fitted with a ribbon blade, spiralize the courgette. Snip any extra-long ribbons in half with scissors.

In a large bowl, mix together the olive oil, thyme and garlic and then season with salt and pepper. Gently stir in the spiralized courgette to coat it in the oil.

Heat a large griddle pan over a high heat. Add the courgette in a single layer and cook for 1–2 minutes, until lightly charred – you may need to do this in 2 batches. Transfer the courgette to a plate and set aside.

Add thc haloumi to the griddle pan and cook for 1–2 minutes on each side, until golden-brown stripes appear and the cheese starts to melt.

Arrange the toasted ciabatta on 2 plates and place the griddled haloumi and courgette on top. Serve immediately.

baked apple and cinnamon crisps

Serves 4–6
Prepare in 5 minutes, plus cooling
Cook in 1¾–2 hours

2 Bramley apples, ends trimmed
1 teaspoon ground cinnamon

I like to use Bramley cooking apples for this recipe but you can also use any large red or green eating apples. The spiralized apples are slowly baked on a low heat to dry them out, which results in a really crisp and tasty snack.

Line 2 large baking sheets with nonstick baking paper. Using a spiralizer fitted with a ribbon blade, spiralize the apples.

Spread out the spiralized apples in a single layer on the prepared baking sheets and sprinkle over the cinnamon.

Bake in a preheated oven, 140°C (275°F), Gas Mark 1, for 1 hour. Turn the crisps and return to the oven for a further 45 minutes–1 hour, until the crisps are lightly golden. Turn off the oven and leave the crisps in the oven to cool and crisp up. The crisps will keep for up to 2 days in an airtight container.

Greek salad pitta pockets

Serves 4
Prepare in 10 minutes

1 small red onion, ends trimmed
12 cm (5 inch) piece cucumber, ends trimmed and cut in half widthways
8 cherry tomatoes, quartered
6 pitted black olives, chopped
125 g (4 oz) feta cheese, crumbled
1 tablepoon lemon juice
2 tablespoons extra virgin olive oil
1 teaspoon dried oregano
4 pitta breads
1 Little Gem lettuce, shredded
salt and freshly ground black pepper

Using a spiralizer fitted with a 3 mm (⅛ inch) spaghetti blade, spiralize the onion and cucumber.

Place the spiralized onion and cucumber in a large bowl with the tomatoes, olives and feta.

In a small bowl, whisk together the lemon juice, oil and oregano and then season to taste with salt and pepper. Pour the dressing over the salad ingredients and gently toss together.

Lightly toast the pittas under a preheated medium-hot grill for about 1 minute on each side.

Slice each pitta bread in half horizontally. Fill the pitta pockets with a little lettuce and then top with the feta mixture. Serve immediately.

mini sweet potato and ricotta frittatas

Makes 8
Prepare in 5 minutes
Cook in 25 minutes

1 large sweet potato, about 250 g (8 oz), peeled, ends trimmed and halved widthways
1 small onion, ends trimmed
1 tablespoon olive oil, plus a little extra for oiling
50 g (2 oz) baby spinach
6 eggs
2 tablespoons chopped sage
1 tablespoon chopped chives
1 teaspoon paprika
125 g (4 oz) ricotta cheese, broken into pieces
salt and freshly ground black pepper
crisp green salad, to serve

Lightly oil 8 holes of a nonstick muffin tin. Using a spiralizer fitted with a 3 mm (⅛ inch) spaghetti blade, spiralize the sweet potato and onion.

Heat the oil in a large frying pan over a medium heat, add the spiralized sweet potato and onion and cook for 3 minutes, until the sweet potato has softened slightly. Add the spinach and cook for 1 minute, until the spinach has wilted. Allow the sweet potato mixture to cool slightly.

Beat the eggs in a large bowl with the herbs and paprika and then season with salt and pepper. Add the sweet potato mixture and mix well. Stir in the ricotta.

Divide the mixture between the holes in the prepared muffin tin and bake in a preheated oven, 180°C (350°F), Gas Mark 4, for 20 minutes or until set. Serve the frittatas immediately with a crisp green salad.

salt and vinegar baked potato crisps

Serves 4
Prepare in 5 minutes, plus standing
Cook in 45 minutes

- 2 potatoes, skins scrubbed and ends trimmed
- 6 tablespoons malt vinegar
- 2 teaspoons sea salt flakes, for sprinkling

Line 2 large baking sheets with nonstick baking paper. Using a spiralizer fitted with a ribbon blade, spiralize the potatoes.

Place the spiralized potatoes in a large bowl and add the vinegar. Toss well to coat in the vinegar and then leave to stand for 30 minutes to allow the potatoes to absorb the flavour.

Drain the potatoes and then lay them out in a single layer on the prepared baking sheets and sprinkle over the salt.

Bake in a preheated oven, 140°C (275 °F), Gas Mark 1, for 30 minutes. Turn the potatoes, removing any crisps that are brown, and return to the oven for a further 15 minutes, until the crisps are lightly golden. Turn off the oven. Return any crisps you removed to the baking sheets and leave the crisps in the oven to cool and crisp up. The crisps will keep for up to 2 days in an airtight container.

crab and vegetable dim sum

Serves 4 as a starter
Prepare in 20 minutes
Cook in 10 minutes

1 carrot (or piece of carrot), about 75 g (3 oz), peeled and ends trimmed
1 courgette (or piece of courgette), about 75 g (3 oz), ends trimmed
125 g (4 oz) fresh or tinned crab meat
2.5 cm (1 inch) piece fresh root ginger, peeled and grated
½ red chilli, deseeded and finely chopped
1 teaspoon toasted sesame oil
2 teaspoons rice wine vinegar
2 teaspoons dark soy sauce
2 teaspoons cornflour
16 dim sum wrappers (available from Asian supermarkets)

To serve
soy sauce
sweet chilli dipping sauce

Using a spiralizer fitted with a 3 mm (⅛ inch) spaghetti blade, spiralize the carrot and courgette. Roughly snip any really long spirals in half with scissors.

Place the spiralized vegetables in a large bowl with all the remaining ingredients, except for the dim sum wrappers. Mix well until thoroughly combined.

Place a dim sum wrapper on a clean surface, brush the edges of the wrapper with a little cold water and place a tablespoon of the crab and vegetable mixture in the centre. Spread out the mixture along the middle and then fold the wrapper over the filling to make a semi-circle. Crimp the edges together with damp hands. Repeat until all the wrappers and the crab and vegetable mixture are used up.

Place half the dim sum in a bamboo or metal steamer over a pan of simmering water and cover with a lid. Steam for 4–5 minutes, until the wrappers are transparent and the filling cooked through. Transfer the dim sum to a warm plate and cover with kitchen foil. Repeat with the remaining dim sum.

Divide the dim sum between 4 plates or arrange on a serving platter and serve immediately with the soy and sweet chilling dipping sauces in dipping bowls alongside.

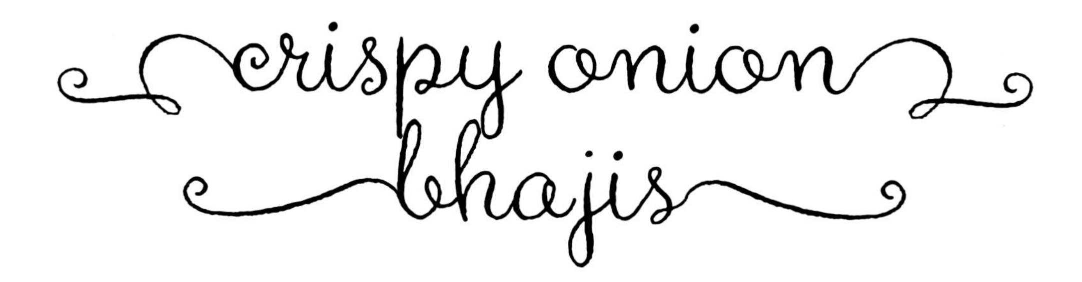

crispy onion bhajis

Makes about 12
Prepare in 10 minutes
Cook in 10 minutes

2 onions, ends trimmed
100 g (3½ oz) gram flour
½ teaspoon baking powder
1 green chilli, finely chopped
2 tablespoons chopped fresh coriander
1 teaspoon salt
1 teaspoon ground cumin
½ teaspoon ground turmeric
1 tablespoon sunflower oil
1 teaspoon lemon juice
5–6 tablespoons water
1 litre (1¾ pints) vegetable or sunflower oil, for deep frying
Cucumber and Mint Raita (see page 92), to serve

Spiralizing onions is really quick and easy, which means that you can make this delicious snack or starter in no time at all.

Using a spiralizer fitted with a 6 mm (¼ inch) flat noodle blade, spiralize the onions.

Place the flour, baking powder, chilli, coriander, salt, cumin and turmeric in a large bowl and mix well. Stir in the sunflower oil, lemon juice and measurement water to make a thick batter. Add the spiralized onions and stir to coat with the batter.

Heat the vegetable or sunflower oil in a wok or deep, heavy-based saucepan to 180–190°C (350–375°F), or until a cube of bread dropped into the oil turns golden brown in 30 seconds. Alternatively, you can use a deep-fat fryer.

Carefully drop tablespoonfuls of the batter into the hot oil, cooking 4 bhajis at a time, and deep-fry for 2–3 minutes, until golden. Remove from the oil with a slotted spoon, drain on kitchen paper and keep warm while you cook the remaining bhaji mixture. Serve the bhajis hot with cucumber and mint raita.

spiral vegetable tempura

Serves 4
Prepare in 10 minutes
Cook in 10–20 minutes

300 g (10 oz) mixed vegetables, such as courgettes, sweet potatoes and carrots, ends trimmed and cut in half widthways
600 ml (1 pint) vegetable oil, for frying
sea salt flakes, for sprinkling

For the batter
200 g (7 oz) plain flour
1 tablespoon cornflour
300 ml (½ pint) cold sparkling water
2 ice cubes

For perfect tempura, make the batter just before cooking and ensure that the oil is the correct temperature so that the batter remains light and crispy.

Using a spiralizer fitted with a ribbon blade, spiralize the vegetables.

Heat the oil in a wok or deep, heavy-based saucepan to 180–190°C (350–375°F), or until a cube of bread dropped into the oil turns golden brown in 30 seconds. Alternatively, you can use a deep-fat fryer.

Meanwhile, make the batter. Place the flour and cornflour in a large bowl and slowly whisk in the water to make a batter about the consistency of double cream. Add the ice cubes to the batter and whisk again.

Dip a few of the vegetable spirals into the batter, shake off any excess and carefully drop the battered vegetables into the hot oil, cooking in batches, and deep-fry for 3–4 minutes, until lightly golden and crisp. Remove the vegetables from the oil with a slotted spoon, drain on kitchen paper and then place on a baking sheet and keep warm in a preheated oven, 150° C (300°F), Gas Mark 2, with the door slightly ajar, to keep crisp. Repeat until you have used up all the vegetables and batter. Sprinkle with salt and serve immediately.

autumn minestrone soup

Serves 4
Prepare in 15 minutes
Cook in 15 minutes

1 onion, ends trimmed
½ small celeriac, peeled and cut into 12 cm (5 inch) chunks
2 carrots, peeled, ends trimmed and halved widthways
1 courgette, ends trimmed and halved widthways
1 tablespoon olive oil
1 garlic clove, crushed
75 g (3 oz) pancetta, cubed
1 x 400 g (13 oz) can chopped tomatoes
750 ml (1¼ pints) hot vegetable stock
⅓ head of Savoy cabbage, thinly sliced
1 x 400 g (13 oz) can borlotti beans, drained and rinsed
salt and freshly ground black pepper

To serve
freshly grated Parmesan cheese
basil leaves
crusty bread

Using a spiralizer fitted with a 3 mm (⅛ inch) spaghetti blade, spiralize the onion, celeriac, carrots and courgette, keeping them separate.

Heat the oil in a large saucepan. Add the spiralized onion and celeriac and the garlic and pancetta and cook over a low heat for 3–4 minutes, until the onion is soft but not browned. Add the spiralized carrots, tomatoes, stock, cabbage and beans, cover and simmer for 5 minutes, or until the celeriac is just tender. Stir in the spiralized courgette, cover and cook for a further 3–4 minutes or until all the vegetables are tender. Season the soup to taste.

Ladle the soup into 4 bowls, sprinkle over the Parmesan and basil leaves and serve with chunks of crusty bread.

smoked haddock chowder

Serves 4
Prepare in 5 minutes
Cook in 15 minutes

1 onion, ends trimmed
225 g (8 oz) potatoes, peeled and ends trimmed
25 g (1 oz) unsalted butter
4 smoked back bacon rashers, trimmed of fat and chopped
450 ml (¾ pint) semi-skimmed milk
300 ml (½ pint) fish stock
150 g (5 oz) canned or frozen sweetcorn
450 g (14½ oz) undyed smoked haddock fillets, skinned and cut into chunky pieces
100 g (3½ oz) baby spinach
freshly ground black pepper
crusty bread, to serve

This creamy chowder is a warming and hearty soup that's packed full of haddock, spiralized potatoes, sweetcorn and wilted baby spinach.

Using a spiralizer fitted with a 3 mm (⅛ inch) spaghetti blade, spiralize the onion. Change to a 6 mm (¼ inch) flat noodle blade and spiralize the potatoes, keeping the onion and potatoes separate.

Melt the butter in a large saucepan over a medium heat. Add the spiralized onion and cook for 2 minutes. Add the bacon and cook for a further 3 minutes, until browned. Pour in the milk and stock, stir in the spiralized potatoes and then bring to the boil. Season well with pepper, reduce the heat, cover and simmer, over a low heat, for 3–4 minutes or until the potatoes are just tender. Stir in the sweetcorn and haddock and gently simmer for 3–4 minutes, until the fish starts to flake. Stir in the spinach.

As soon as the spinach has wilted, ladle the soup into bowls. Serve with crusty bread.

pumpkin, cheese and chive muffins

Makes 10
Prepare in 10 minutes
Cook in 20–25 minutes

large chunk of pumpkin or butternut squash (the non-bulbous end), about 275 g (9 oz), peeled
275 g (9 oz) plain flour
1 tablespoon baking powder
125 g (4 oz) mature Cheddar cheese, grated
2 tablespoons chopped chives
2 eggs
175 ml (6 fl oz) milk
75 g (3 oz) butter, melted
2 tablespoons pumpkin seeds

Line a muffin tin with 10 paper muffin cases. Using a spiralizer fitted with a 3 mm (⅛ inch) spaghetti blade, spiralize the pumpkin or squash. Roughly snip any long strands in half with scissors.

In a large bowl, sift together the flour and baking powder. Stir in the cheese and chives and mix well.

In a separate bowl, beat together the eggs, milk and melted butter.

Pour the wet ingredients over the dry ingredients and stir until just combined. Stir in the spiralized pumpkin or squash.

Divide the mixture between the muffin cases and then sprinkle the tops with the pumpkin seeds. Bake in a preheated oven,190°C (375°F), Gas Mark 5, for 20–25 minutes, until risen and firm. These muffins are delicious served both warm and cold.

baked vegetable crisps

Serves 4
Prepare in 10 minutes
Cook in 30–35 minutes

1 sweet potato, peeled, ends trimmed and halved widthways
1 large parsnip, peeled, ends trimmed and halved widthways
2 fresh beetroot, scrubbed and ends trimmed
2 tablespoons olive oil
sea salt flakes

These colourful oven-baked vegetable crisps make a healthy alternative to deep-fried potato crisps. Any leftovers can be stored for 1–2 days in an airtight container.

Line 2 large baking sheets with nonstick baking paper. Using a spiralizer fitted with a ribbon blade, spiralize the sweet potato, parsnip and beetroot.

Place the spiralized vegetables in a large bowl, drizzle with the oil, sprinkle with a little sea salt and mix well.

Spread out the vegetables in a single layer on the prepared baking sheets. Bake in a preheated oven, 160°C (325°F), Gas Mark 3, for 30–35 minutes, turning the vegetables and swapping over the baking sheets in the oven halfway through the cooking time, until the crisps are lightly golden and crispy. (Remove any crisps that are already golden when you turn over the vegetables.)

Turn off the oven. Return any crisps you removed to the baking sheets and leave the crisps in the oven to cool and crisp up – the crisps will become extra crispy as they cool. Sprinkle with a little extra sea salt and serve.

salads

chicken, courgette and quinoa salad

Serves 4
Prepare in 10 minutes
Cook in 20–30 minutes

200 g (7 oz) quinoa, rinsed
2 courgettes, ends trimmed and halved widthways
1 tablespoon olive oil
2 teaspoons sumac
3 boneless, skinless chicken breasts
finely grated rind and juice of 1 large unwaxed lemon
1 tablespoon extra virgin olive oil
4 tablespoons chopped mint
100 g (3½ oz) pistachios, roughly chopped
150 g (5 oz) pomegranate seeds
salt and freshly ground black pepper

Griddling the courgette ribbons gives them a lovely smoky flavour. Be careful not to overcook the courgettes or they will lose their texture.

Place the quinoa in a saucepan, cover with 600 ml (1 pint) cold water and add a little salt. Bring to the boil, then reduce the heat and simmer for 10–15 minutes or until the quinoa is tender and has absorbed most of the water. Remove from the heat, cover and leave to stand while you prepare the rest of the salad.

Using a spiralizer fitted with a ribbon blade, spiralize the courgettes.

Place the olive oil and sumac in shallow dish and season with salt and pepper. Add the chicken and toss to coat.

Heat a griddle pan until hot. Add the chicken and cook over a medium heat for 4– 6 minutes on each side or until cooked through. Transfer the chicken to a plate and set aside.

Add the spiralized courgettes to the griddle pan and cook for about 2 minutes or until lightly charred.

Place the quinoa in a large bowl, add the lemon rind and juice, extra virgin olive oil, mint and pistachios, mix well and season to taste. Gently stir in the courgettes and pomegranate seeds.

Thinly slice the chicken breasts. Divide the quinoa salad between 4 plates, top with the chicken and serve immediately.

Japanese tuna tataki salad

Serves 2 as a main meal or 4 as a starter
Prepare in 20 minutes
Cook in 2 minutes

250 g (8 oz) daikon, peeled, ends trimmed and halved widthways
½ cucumber, ends trimmed and halved widthways
2 tablespoons sesame seeds
1 tablespoon black peppercorns
pinch of salt
2 x 175 g (6 oz) tuna steaks, about 2.5 cm (1 inch) thick
1 tablespoon sunflower oil
wasabi paste, to serve

For the dressing
2 tablespoons Japanese soy sauce
finely grated rind and juice of 1 unwaxed lime
1 teaspoon grated fresh root ginger
2 teaspoons yuzu citrus juice (or use grapefruit juice)
2 tablespoons mirin
1 tablespoon honey

Using a spiralizer fitted with a 3 mm (⅛ inch) spaghetti blade, spiralize the cucumber and daikon. Place the spiralized vegetables in a bowl of ice-cold water and place in the refrigerator.

Now make the dressing. Whisk together all the dressing ingredients in a small bowl.

Toast the sesame seeds in a dry frying pan over a medium heat for 2 minutes, until just golden. Allow to cool.

Roughly crush the peppercorns in a pestle with a mortar, then add the toasted sesame seeds and a pinch of salt and grind until everything is roughly crushed.

Tip the sesame mixture onto a plate and spread out. Gently press the tuna steaks into the sesame mixture, turning over and repeating until evenly coated.

Heat the oil in a large nonstick frying pan over a medium heat. Fry the tuna steaks for 1 minute on each side, until the outside is cooked but the middle is still pink. Remove from the pan and set aside to rest.

Drain the cucumber and daikon and pat dry with kitchen paper. Divide the vegetables between 4 plates or place on a large platter.

Thinly slice the tuna and arrange on top of the cucumber and daikon. Drizzle over some of the dressing and serve immediately with the remaining dressing and wasabi paste alongside.

butternut squash, feta and Puy lentil salad

Serves 4
Prepare in 10 minutes
Cook in 20 minutes

½ butternut squash (the non-bulbous end), about 500 g (1 lb), peeled and halved widthways.
3 tablespoons olive oil
1 teaspoon cumin seeds
juice of 1 small lemon
1 teaspoon Dijon mustard
250 g (8 oz) ready-to-eat Puy lentils
25 g (1 oz) walnuts pieces
125 g (4 oz) feta cheese, crumbled
100 g (3½ oz) baby spinach
salt and freshly ground black pepper

Using a spiralizer fitted with a 3 mm (⅛ inch) spaghetti blade, spiralize the squash.

Place the spiralized squash in a large bowl, add 1 tablespoon of the oil and the cumin seeds and season with salt and pepper. Mix well to coat the squash in the oil, cumin seeds and seasoning.

Spread out the squash on a large nonstick baking sheet and roast in a preheated oven, 190°C (375°F), Gas Mark 5, for about 20 minutes, stirring halfway through, until golden and starting to crisp. Remove from the oven and leave to cool slightly.

In a small bowl, whisk together the remaining oil with the lemon juice and mustard and season to taste with salt and pepper.

Place the squash and all the remaining ingredients in a large bowl, pour over the lemon and mustard mixture and gently toss together. Serve immediately in bowls.

Thai beef salad

Serves 4
Prepare in 15 minutes
Cook in 10–15 minutes

1 small cucumber, ends trimmed and halved widthways
2 carrots, peeled, ends trimmed and halved widthways
1 mooli, peeled, ends trimmed and halved widthways
500 g (1 lb) rump steak
1 tablespoon sunflower or groundnut oil
½ head of Chinese leaf or Iceberg lettuce, finely sliced
handful of peanuts, roughly chopped (optional)
salt and freshly ground black pepper

For the dressing
2 tablespoons palm or soft brown sugar
2 tablespoons fish sauce
juice of 3 limes
3 garlic cloves, crushed
1 bird's eye chilli, deseeded and finely chopped
6 tablespoons chopped fresh coriander

First, make the dressing. Whisk together all the dressing ingredients in a small bowl until the sugar has dissolved.

Using a spiralizer fitted with a 3 mm (⅛ inch) spaghetti blade, spiralize the cucumber, carrots and mooli.

Place the spiralized vegetables in a bowl and pour over half the dressing. Leave the salad to marinate while you cook the beef.

Brush the steak with the oil and season with salt and pepper. Heat a griddle pan until smoking hot, then add the steak and cook over a medium-high heat for 3–6 minutes on each side, or until cooked to your liking. Transfer the steak to a plate and allow to rest for 5 minutes, then thinly slice.

Just before you are ready to serve, stir the Chinese leaf or lettuce into the salad. Divide the salad between 4 plates or place on a large platter or board, top with the beef and drizzle over the remaining dressing. Sprinkle over the peanuts, if using, and serve immediately.

Jerusalem artichoke and bacon salad

Serves 4
Prepare in 12 minutes
Cook in 10 minutes

2 tablespoons olive oil
8 smoked back bacon rashers, chopped
1 garlic clove, crushed
350 g (12 oz) large Jerusalem artichokes, scrubbed
2 tablespoons flat leaf parsley
2 tablespoons balsamic vinegar
1 tablespoon lemon juice
8 Little Gem lettuces, quartered
a small handful of Parmesan cheese shavings
salt and freshly ground black pepper

Heat 1 tablespoon of the oil in a large frying pan or wok over a medium heat. Add the bacon and garlic and cook for 2–3 minutes, stirring occasionally, until the bacon is lightly coloured.

Meanwhile, using a spiralizer fitted with a ribbon blade, spiralize the Jerusalem artichokes. Snip any extra-long ribbons in half with scissors.

Immediately add the spiralized artichokes to the bacon in the frying pan (to prevent the artichokes discolouring) and stir-fry for 3–4 minutes, until the bacon and artichokes start to turn crispy. Remove from the heat and stir in the parsley.

In a small bowl, whisk together the remaining oil, the vinegar and lemon juice and season to taste with salt and pepper.

Divide the lettuce between 4 plates and top with the warm bacon and artichoke mixture. Spoon over a little of the dressing, sprinkle with Parmesan shavings and serve immediately.

smoked salmon salad ~with dill and lemon~

Serves 4
Prepare in 10 minutes, plus marinating

1 large fennel bulb, ends trimmed
1 courgette, ends trimmed and halved widthways
½ cucumber, ends trimmed and halved widthways
2 teaspoons finely chopped dill
2 tablespoons lemon juice
1 tablespoon olive oil
1 teaspoon caster sugar
½ teaspoon sea salt flakes
8 slices smoked salmon
lemon wedges, to serve

This tasty salad combines spiralized crunchy vegetables in a dill and lemony dressing with delicious smoked salmon. It is great as a main meal or starter.

Using a spiralizer fitted with a ribbon blade, spiralize the fennel, courgette and cucumber. Pat the cucumber dry on kitchen paper.

Place the spiralized vegetables in a large bowl and add the dill, lemon juice, oil, sugar and salt. Toss well to combine and leave to marinate for 10 minutes.

Divide the vegetables between 4 plates, top with the salmon and serve immediately with lemon wedges to squeeze over.

smoked mackerel and quails' egg salad

Serves 4
Prepare in 10 minutes
Cook in 20 minutes

12 quails' eggs
175 g (6 oz) watercress or rocket leaves
375 g (12 oz) smoked peppered mackerel fillets, skin removed and broken into large flakes
16 cherry tomatoes, halved

For the crispy potato straws
2 potatoes, peeled and ends trimmed
1 tablespoon olive oil
salt and freshly ground black pepper

For the dressing
2 tablespoons olive oil
2 teaspoons wholegrain mustard
1 tablespoon white wine vinegar
1 teaspoon honey
1 tablespoon chopped chives

The potato straws provide a lovely crisp contrast in this salad. You can replace the quails' eggs with 4 chickens' eggs, if you prefer, increasing the cooking time for the eggs to 6–8 minutes.

First, make the crispy potato straws. Using a spiralizer fitted with a 3 mm (1/8 inch) spaghetti blade, spiralize the potatoes. Place the spiralized potatoes in a large bowl, add the oil, season with salt and pepper and toss together to coat. Line a large baking sheet with baking paper and arrange the potatoes on the baking sheet in a single layer. Bake in a preheated oven, 180°C (350°F), Gas Mark 4, for 10 minutes, then turn the potatoes, removing any potatoes that are cooked, and bake for a further 10 minutes or until golden and crispy. Allow to cool.

Meanwhile, cook the quails' eggs in a saucepan of boiling water for 3 minutes. Drain the eggs, refresh in cold water, then shell and halve them.

To make the dressing, whisk together the oil, mustard, vinegar and honey in a small bowl. Season to taste and stir in the chives.

Toss the watercress or rocket leaves with a little of the dressing and divide between 4 plates. Top with the smoked mackerel, quails' eggs and tomatoes, drizzle over the remaining dressing and top with the crispy potato straws. Serve immediately.

apple, chicory and walnut salad

Serves 2
Prepare in 10 minutes

1 large red eating apple, ends trimmed
1 head of white chicory, leaves separated
1 head of red chicory, leaves separated
50 g (2 oz) watercress
25 g (1 oz) walnuts, chopped
salt and freshly ground black pepper

For the dressing
juice of ½ lemon
1 tablespoon walnut or light olive oil
1 teaspoon Dijon mustard
1 teaspoon honey

The sweetness of the apple perfectly balances the bitterness of the chicory in this simple salad. Serve it on its own or as an accompaniment for grilled meat.

First make the dressing. In a small bowl, whisk together all the dressing ingredients and then season to taste with a little salt and pepper.

Using a spiralizer fitted with a ribbon blade, spiralize the apple.

Arrange the spiralized apple, chicory and watercress on a large platter. Drizzle over the dressing and gently toss together. Sprinkle over the walnuts and serve immediately.

green papaya and chicken salad

Serves 4
Prepare in 15 minutes, plus marinating

1 large green papaya, about 650 g (1 lb 5 oz), peeled and ends trimmed
4 spring onions, finely sliced
250 g (8 oz) cooked skinless chicken breasts, shredded
4 tablespoons chopped fresh coriander
small handful of mint leaves, to garnish
lime wedges, to serve

For the dressing
juice of 2 limes
1 teaspoon palm or soft brown sugar
1 red chilli, deseeded and finely chopped
2 teaspoons finely grated fresh root ginger
2 teaspoons dark soy sauce

Green, or unripe, papaya are long green fruit that are now readily available in supermarkets and Asian stores. The strips of papaya and shredded chicken in this light and fragrant Thai-style salad soak up the delicious chilli and lime dressing beautifully.

Cut the papaya in half widthways and tap out the seeds. Attach the narrow end of one half of the papaya to a spiralizer fitted with a 3 mm (⅛ inch) spaghetti blade and spiralize the papaya. Repeat with the remaining papaya half.

Place all the dressing ingredients in a small bowl and whisk until the sugar has dissolved.

Place the spiralized papaya in a large bowl, add the spring onions and shredded chicken and pour over the dressing. Toss well and leave to marinate for about 10 minutes. Stir in the coriander. Garnish the salad with mint leaves and serve with lime wedges to squeeze over.

Vietnamese chicken and noodle salad

Serves 4
Prepare in 10 minutes

150 g (5 oz) instant rice vermicelli noodles
2 carrots, peeled, ends trimmed and halved widthways
½ cucumber, ends trimmed
250 g (8 oz) cooked skinless chicken breasts, shredded
75 g (3 oz) bean sprouts
4 tablespoons chopped mint
4 tablespoons chopped fresh coriander
50 g (2 oz) roasted peanuts, chopped

For the dressing
2 tablespoons rice wine vinegar
3 tablespoons sweet chili sauce
1 tablespoon Thai fish sauce
4 tablespoons lime juice

To garnish
coriander leaves
mint leaves

Place the noodles in a large bowl and pour over boiling water to cover. Leave to stand for 3 minutes, then refresh under cold water and leave to drain.

Meanwhile, using a spiralizer fitted with a 6 mm (¼ inch) flat noodle blade, spiralize the carrots and cucumber.

Place the spiralized vegetables in a large bowl with the chicken, bean sprouts, chopped herbs, peanuts and noodles.

In a small bowl, whisk together the dressing ingredients.

Pour the dressing over the noodle salad and toss well. Divide the salad between 4 bowls, garnish with coriander and mint leaves and serve immediately.

pear, ham and blue cheese salad

Serves 2
Prepare in 5 minutes

1 large or 2 small red-skinned pears, pointy ends trimmed
juice of 1 lemon
1 tablespoon extra virgin olive oil
100 g (3½ oz) rocket leaves
4 slices Serrano ham
75 g (3 oz) Roquefort or dolcelatte cheese, cubed
salt and freshly ground black pepper

The red-skinned pears are very pretty but you can use green-skinned pears if you prefer. The crunchy texture of the pears works really well with the creamy blue cheese.

Using a spiralizer fitted with a 6 mm (¼ inch) flat noodle blade, spiralize the pears. Place the spiralized pears in a bowl and spoon over a little of the lemon juice, to prevent them going brown.

To make a dressing, whisk together the remaining lemon juice and the oil in a small bowl and season with salt and pepper.

Divide the rocket leaves between 2 plates, top with the pear and slices of ham and scatter over the cheese. Drizzle with the dressing and serve immediately.

beetroot, smoked trout and horseradish salad

Serves 2
Prepare in 10 minutes

- 2 fresh beetroot, scrubbed and ends trimmed
- 2 tablespoons reduced-fat crème fraîche
- 2 tablespoons 0% Greek yogurt
- 1 tablespoon creamed horseradish sauce
- 2 teaspoons white wine vinegar
- 100 g (3½ oz) watercress
- 250 g (8 oz) hot-smoked trout fillets, flaked into large pieces
- freshly ground black pepper

Raw beetroot contains lots of vitamin C and iron, which will give your immune system a boost.

Using a spiralizer fitted with a 3 mm (⅛ inch) spaghetti blade, spiralize the beetroot.

In a large bowl, mix together the crème fraîche, yogurt, horseradish sauce and vinegar. Add the spiralized beetroot and gently stir until evenly coated.

Divide the watercress between 2 plates, top with the beetroot and arrange the trout over the top. Sprinkle over some pepper and serve immediately.

mains

butternut squash, sage and goats' cheese tart

Serves 6–8
Prepare in 10 minutes
Cook in 1 hour

350g (11½ oz) ready-made shortcrust pastry
½ butternut squash (the non-bulbous end), about 500g (1 lb), peeled and halved widthways
1 tablespoon olive oil
4 smoked back bacon rashers, chopped
1 garlic clove, crushed
150 g (5 oz) goats' cheese, roughly chopped
300 ml (½ pint) double cream
3 eggs
8 sage leaves
salt and freshly ground black pepper

On a lightly floured surface, roll out the pastry until large enough to fit a 25 cm (10 inch) loose-bottomed tart tin. Line the tin with the pastry. Prick the base with a fork, cover with nonstick baking paper and fill with baking beans. Place the tin on a baking sheet and bake in a preheated oven, 190°C (375°F), Gas Mark 5, for 15 minutes. Remove the baking beans and paper and return to the oven for 5 minutes, until golden.

Meanwhile, using a spiralizer fitted with a 3 mm (⅛ inch) spaghetti blade, spiralize the squash. You should end up with about 375 g (12 oz) spiralized squash.

Heat the oil in a large frying pan and cook the bacon over a medium heat for 2–3 minutes, until coloured. Add the garlic and cook for 1 minute, then add the squash and stir-fry for 2–3 minutes, until slightly softened. Arrange the squash mixture in the pastry case and scatter over half the goats' cheese.

Beat together the cream and eggs in a bowl and then season with salt and pepper. Pour the egg mixture over the butternut squash. Sprinkle with the remaining goats' cheese and the sage leaves.

Bake for 40 minutes, until the top is golden and the filling set. Leave to cool for 5 minutes, then cut the tart into slices and serve.

cottage pie with crispy topping

Serves 4
Prepare in 10 minutes
Cook in 40–50 minutes

1 onion, ends trimmed
2 carrots, peeled, ends trimmed and halved widthways
500 g (1 lb) minced beef
1 tablespoon plain flour
300 ml (½ pint) hot beef stock
1 tablespoon tomato purée
1 tablespoon Worcestershire sauce
1 tablespoon dried mixed herbs
steamed shredded green cabbage, to serve

For the crispy topping
2 parsnips, peeled and ends trimmed
2 large potatoes, peeled, ends trimmed and halved widthways
100 g (3½ oz) mature Cheddar cheese, grated

Using a spiralizer fitted with a 3 mm (⅛ inch) spaghetti blade, spiralize the onion and carrots, keeping them separate.

Place the mince and spiralized onion in a large saucepan and dry-fry over a medium heat for 3–4 minutes, until the mince is browned. Add the spiralized carrots and stir in the flour, cook for 1 minute and then stir in all the remaining ingredients. Bring to the boil, reduce the heat, partially cover and simmer for 15–20 minutes, until the liquid has reduced and thickened.

Meanwhile, make the topping. Using a spiralizer fitted with a 3 mm (⅛ inch) spaghetti blade, spiralize the parsnips and potatoes. Place the spiralized parsnips and potatoes in a saucepan of boiling water and cook for 2–3 minutes, until just tender. Drain well and allow to cool slightly. Transfer the parsnips and potatoes to a large bowl, add the cheese and stir to mix well.

Transfer the mince mixture to a 1.5 litre (2½ pint) ovenproof dish and cover with the topping. Bake in a preheated oven, 180°C (350°F), Gas Mark 4, for 20–25 minutes, until the topping is crispy and the mince bubbling. Serve with some steamed shredded green cabbage.

courgetti with crab, chilli and lemon

Serves 2
Prepare in 5 minutes
Cook in 5 minutes

2 large courgettes, ends trimmed and halved widthways
1 tablespoon olive oil
1 garlic clove, crushed
1 small red chilli, deseeded and finely chopped
100 g (3½ oz) fresh white crab meat
finely grated rind and juice of ½ unwaxed lemon
1 tablespoon chopped mint
freshly ground black pepper

Using a spiralizer fitted with a 3 mm (⅛ inch) spaghetti blade, spiralize the courgettes.

Heat the oil in a wok or large frying pan, add the garlic and chilli and cook gently over a medium heat for 2 minutes. Stir in the spiralized courgettes and cook for 2–3 minutes, until just tender. Stir in the crab, lemon rind and juice and mint, gently toss together and season with pepper. Serve immediately.

chicken traybake with sweet potatoes

Serves 4
Prepare in 10 minutes
Cook in 30–35 minutes

finely grated rind and juice of 2 unwaxed lemons, reserving the squeezed lemon halves
1 tablespoon dried oregano
2 teaspoons dried thyme
2 teaspoons smoked paprika
100 ml (3½ fl oz) white wine or chicken stock
2 tablespoons olive oil
400 g (13 oz) sweet potatoes, peeled and ends trimmed
4 chicken thighs
4 chicken drumsticks
6 garlic cloves, unpeeled
14 pitted green olives
salt and freshly ground black pepper
steamed green beans or broccoli, to serve

The spiralized sweet potatoes cook really quickly in this traybake recipe, making it the ideal dish for a speedy midweek supper.

In a large jug, mix together the lemon rind and juice, dried herbs, paprika, white wine or stock and olive oil and season well with salt and pepper.

Using a spiralizer fitted with a 3 mm (⅛ inch) spaghetti blade, spiralize the sweet potatoes.

Place the chicken, spiralized sweet potatoes and garlic cloves in a large roasting tin. Pour the lemony mixture over the chicken and potatoes and mix everything together until well coated. Arrange the chicken pieces, skin-side up on the top of the sweet potatoes and tuck in the reserved squeezed lemon halves.

Roast in a preheated oven, 190°C (375°F), Gas Mark 5, for 20 minutes. Baste the chicken and potatoes with the lemony sauce and add the olives. Return to the oven and cook for a further 10–15 minutes or until the chicken is golden brown and potatoes tender. Serve with some steamed green beans or broccoli.

curried sweet potato puffs

Makes 6
Prepare in 10 minutes
Cook in 25–30 minutes

1 onion, ends trimmed
2 sweet potatoes, about 400g (13 oz), peeled, ends trimmed and halved widthways
1 tablespoon sunflower oil
2 tablespoons Thai red curry paste
4 tablespoons coconut cream
2 tablespoons chopped fresh coriander
plain flour, for dusting
375 g (12 oz) ready-made, all-butter puff pastry
1 beaten egg, to glaze
salt and freshly ground black pepper

Using a spiralizer fitted with a 3 mm (⅛ inch) spaghetti blade, spiralize the onion and sweet potatoes, keeping them separate.

Heat the oil in a large saucepan or frying pan with a lid. Add the spiralized onion and cook over a medium heat for 1–2 minutes, until softened. Stir in the curry paste and cook for 1 minute, then add the coconut cream, stir and then add the spiralized sweet potatoes. Cover and simmer for 2–3 minutes, until the sweet potatoes start to soften. Allow the mixture to cool slightly and then stir in the coriander and season to taste with salt and pepper.

On a lightly-floured surface, roll out the pastry until about 5 mm (¼ inch) thick. Cut out 6 x 15 cm (6 inch) rounds. Divide the sweet potato mixture between the pastry circles, piling it along the centre of each circle. Brush the edges of the pastry with a little beaten egg and then fold over the pastry to cover the filling and form a semi-circle. Pinch or crimp the edges together between your forefinger and thumb to seal.

Transfer the parcels to a nonstick baking sheet, gently prick the sides of the pastry with a fork and then brush the parcels with the beaten egg. Bake in a preheated oven, 190°C (375°F), Gas Mark 5, for 20 minutes, until puffed and golden. These sweet potato puffs are delicious served both hot and cold.

butternut squash with sage and pine nuts

Serves 2
Prepare in 5 minutes
Cook in 10 minutes

½ butternut squash (the non-bulbous end), about 500g (1 lb), peeled and halved widthways
25 g (1 oz) unsalted butter
8 sage leaves
25g (1 oz) pine nuts
25 g (1 oz) Parmesan cheese, grated
freshly ground black pepper
crisp green salad, to serve

Using a spiralizer fitted with a 3 mm (⅛ inch) spaghetti blade, spiralize the squash. You should end up with about 375 g (12 oz) spiralized squash.

Place the butter in a large frying pan over a medium heat. When the butter starts to foam, stir in the sage leaves and pine nuts and cook for 1–2 minutes, until the sage is crispy and the pine nuts are lightly golden. Add the squash and stir-fry for 5–6 minutes or until the squash is tender. Remove from the heat and stir in half the Parmesan.

Divide the squash between 2 bowls, sprinkle with the remaining Parmesan and season with plenty of pepper. Serve with a crisp green salad.

prawn pad Thai

Serves 2
Prepare in 15 minutes
Cook in 10 minutes

1 mooli, about 375 g (12 oz), peeled, ends trimmed and halved widthways
1 carrot, ends trimmed and halved widthways
2 tablespoons groundnut or sunflower oil
1 garlic clove, chopped
1 red chilli, deseeded and finely chopped
1 bunch of spring onions, sliced
125 g (4 oz) raw shelled prawns
2 eggs, beaten
200 g (7 oz) bean sprouts
4 lime wedges, to serve

For the noodle sauce
2 tablespoons tamarind paste
2 tablespoons fish sauce
2 tablespoons palm or soft brown sugar
juice of 1 lime

To garnish
2 tablespoons blanched peanuts, toasted and roughly chopped
4 tablespoons chopped fresh coriander

This recipe for pad Thai replaces traditional flat rice noodles with spiralized mooli, making it an ideal dish for those on a low-carb diet.

First, make the noodle sauce. In a small bowl, whisk together the tamarind paste, fish sauce, sugar and lime juice.

Using a spiralizer fitted with a 6 mm (¼ inch) flat noodle blade, spiralize the mooli. Change to a 3 mm (⅛ inch) spaghetti blade and spiralize the carrot, keeping the mooli and carrot separate.

Heat a wok over a high heat, then add 1 tablespoon of the oil and swirl around. Add the garlic, chilli and spring onions and stir-fry for 1 minute, stirring continuously. Add the spiralized mooli and stir-fry for 2 minutes, then add the spiralized carrots and prawns and stir-fry for 1–2 minutes or until the prawns have turned pink.

Push the stir-fried ingredients to the side of the wok and add the remaining oil. Pour in the eggs and cook, stirring continuously, until they begin to set.

Add the bean sprouts and pour over the noodle sauce. Toss everything together and heat through, stirring continuously for 2 minutes. Stir in half the garnish, then spoon into bowls and sprinkle with the remaining garnish. Serve immediately with lime wedges to squeeze over.

Spanish chorizo tortilla

Serves 6
Prepare in 10 minutes
Cook in 20–25 minutes

1 large onion, ends trimmed
450 g (14½ oz) potatoes, peeled and ends trimmed
2 tablespoons olive oil
175 g (6 oz) chorizo, diced
5 eggs
2 tablespoons flat leaf parsley
salt and freshly ground black pepper
1 teaspoon smoked paprika, for sprinkling

A tortilla made with spiralized potatoes will cook more quickly than a traditional tortilla made with sliced potatoes.

Using a spiralizer fitted with a 3 mm (⅛ inch) spaghetti blade, spiralize the onion and potatoes, keeping them separate.

Heat 1 tablespoon of the olive oil in a 20 cm (8 inch) nonstick frying pan with a lid. Gently cook the chorizo and spiralized onion over a medium heat for 2–3 minutes, until the onion has softened and the paprika has been released from the chorizo. Add the spiralized potatoes and stir to coat in the paprika and onion mixture. Cover and cook for 5 minutes, turning the potatoes once and shaking the pan from time to time, until the potatoes are just tender.

In a large bowl, beat together the eggs and parsley and season with salt and pepper. Add the potato mixture and stir thoroughly to combine.

Heat the remaining oil in the frying pan and pour in the egg and potato mixture. Cook over a low heat for 8–10 minutes, without stirring, until set.

Place the frying pan under a preheated hot grill and cook for 2–3 minutes, until the top of the tortilla is golden brown.

Transfer the tortilla to a board. Sprinkle the tortilla with the smoked paprika, cut into wedges and serve.

sesame and ginger salmon en papilotte

Serves 2
Prepare in 10 minutes
Cook in 12–15 minutes

2.5 cm (1 inch) piece fresh root ginger, peeled and cut into thin matchsticks
2 tablespoons light soy sauce
2 tablespoons Chinese rice wine vinegar
1 teaspoon toasted sesame oil
1 carrot, peeled, ends trimmed and halved widthways
1 courgette, ends trimmed and halved widthways
4 spring onions, thinly sliced
2 skinless salmon fillets, about 200 g (7 oz) each
2 teaspoons sesame seeds, toasted
steamed rice, to serve

The spiralized carrot and courgette will steam perfectly in the paper parcel with the salmon and ginger.

In a small bowl, mix together the ginger, soy sauce, rice wine vinegar and sesame oil to make a sauce.

Using a spiralizer fitted with a 3 mm (1/8 inch) spaghetti blade, spiralize the carrot and courgette.

Place 2 x 23 cm (9 inch) squares of baking paper on a large baking sheet. Divide the spiralized vegetables and the spring onions between the 2 sheets of baking paper and then place a salmon fillet on top of each pile of vegetables. Spoon over the sauce and then sprinkle with the sesame seeds. Fold over the paper to seal the parcel.

Place the parcels on a baking sheet and bake in a preheated oven, 200°C (400°F), Gas Mark 6, for 12–15 minutes, until the salmon is opaque and the fish flakes easily. Transfer the parcels to plates, carefully open up the parcels and serve with steamed rice.

easy potato moussaka

Serves 4
Prepare in 10 minutes
Cook in 50–55 minutes

1 large onion, ends trimmed
500 g (1 lb) minced lamb
1 garlic clove, crushed
1 teaspoon ground cinnamon
2 teaspoons dried oregano
150 ml (¼ pint) red wine or lamb stock
1 x 400 g (13 oz) can chopped tomatoes
2 tablespoons tomato purée
500 g (1 lb) potatoes, peeled and ends trimmed
300 g (10 oz) 0% Greek yogurt
2 eggs, beaten
125 g (4 oz) reduced-fat mature Cheddar cheese, grated
crisp green salad, to serve

This family meal is quick to prepare and contains a lot less fat than a traditional moussaka made with aubergines.

Using a spiralizer fitted with a 3 mm (⅛ inch) spaghetti blade, spiralize the onion.

Place the mince, spiralized onion and garlic in a large saucepan and dry-fry for 3–4 minutes, until browned. Stir in the cinnamon, oregano, wine or stock, tomatoes and tomato purée, bring to the boil, then cover and simmer for 15 minutes.

Meanwhile, using a spiralizer fitted with a ribbon blade, spiralize the potatoes. Place the spiralized potatoes in a saucepan of slightly salted boiling water and simmer for 3–4 minutes, until just tender. Drain well.

In a small bowl, whisk together the yogurt and eggs until smooth and then stir in most of the cheese.

Place half of the lamb mixture in the bottom of a 1.5 litre (2½ pint) ovenproof dish. Cover with half the potatoes and then repeat the layers, finishing with a layer of potatoes. Spoon the yogurt mixture over the top of the potatoes and sprinkle with the remaining cheese.

Bake the moussaka in a preheated oven, 180°C (350°F), Gas Mark 4, for 25–30 minutes, until golden and bubbling. Serve with a crisp green salad.

spicy baked cod with potato topping

Serves 2
Prepare in 10 minutes
Cook in 40–45 minutes

1 onion, ends trimmed
2 tablespoons sunflower oil
1 garlic clove, crushed
2.5 cm (1 inch) piece fresh root ginger, peeled and chopped
2 tablespoons tikka or medium curry paste
1 tablespoon lemon juice
1 x 400 g (13 oz) can chopped tomatoes
150 ml (¼ pint) vegetable stock
200 g (7 oz) baby spinach
2 tablespoons chopped fresh coriander
2 potatoes, about 500 g (1 lb), peeled, ends trimmed and halved widthways
2 skinless chunky cod loins, about 150–175 g (5–6 oz) each
salt and freshly ground black pepper

Using a spiralizer fitted with a 3 mm (⅛ inch) spaghetti blade, spiralize the onion.

Heat 1 tablespoon of the oil in a large saucepan and cook the spiralized onion, garlic and ginger over a medium heat for 2–3 minutes, until softened. Stir in the curry paste and cook for 1 minute. Add the lemon juice, tomatoes and stock and season with salt and pepper. Bring to the boil, then cover and simmer for 5 minutes. Stir in the spinach and coriander and remove from the heat.

Using a spiralizer fitted with a 3 mm (⅛ inch) spaghetti blade, spiralize the potatoes. Place the spiralized potatoes on a clean tea towel or kitchen paper and gently squeeze out any excess liquid. Pat the potatoes dry with kitchen paper.

Place the spiralized potatoes in a large bowl, add the remaining oil and season with salt and pepper. Stir to coat the potatoes in the oil and seasoning.

Pour the curry mixture into the base of a 1.2 litre (2 pint) ovenproof dish, arrange the cod loins on top and cover the cod with the potatoes. Bake in a preheated oven, 180°C (350°F), Gas Mark 4, for 30–35 minutes or until the potatoes are crispy and tender and the cod is cooked through.

butternut squash with ricotta and herbs

Serves 2
Prepare in 5 minutes
Cook in 10 minutes

½ coquina or butternut squash (the non-bulbous end), about 500 g (1 lb), peeled and halved widthways
125 g (4 oz) ricotta cheese
2 tablespoons chopped fresh herbs, such as parsley, chives and basil
finely grated rind and juice of 1 small unwaxed lemon
1 tablespoon sunflower oil
1 garlic clove, crushed
100 g (3½ oz) baby spinach
100 g (3½ oz) frozen peas
salt and freshly ground black pepper
freshly grated Parmesan cheese, to serve

Using a spiralizer fitted with a 3 mm (⅛ inch) spaghetti blade, spiralize the squash.

In a small bowl, mix together the ricotta, herbs and lemon rind and juice to make a sauce.

Heat the oil in a large wok or frying pan over a medium heat. Add the garlic and cook for 1 minute, then stir in the spiralized squash and stir-fry for about 5 minutes or until the squash starts to soften but is not breaking up. Stir in the spinach and peas and cook for 2 minutes, until the spinach has wilted.

Add the ricotta and herb sauce and 4 tablespoons boiling water, stir and cook for a further 1–2 minutes until the sauce has coated the squash. Season to taste with salt and pepper, sprinkle some Parmesan over the top and serve immediately.

Moroccan turkey burgers

Serves 6
Prepare in 10 minutes, plus chilling
Cook in 15 minutes

For the burgers

1 large courgette, ends trimmed and halved widthways
500 g (1lb) lean turkey or chicken breast mince
4 spring onions, chopped
1 garlic clove, crushed
2 tablespoons chopped mint
2 tablespoons chopped fresh coriander
1 tablespoon harissa paste
2 teaspoons ground cumin
1 egg, beaten
1 teaspoon salt
freshly ground black pepper
1 tablespoon sunflower oil, for brushing

For the sumac yogurt dip

200 g (7 oz) 0% Greek yogurt
1 garlic clove, crushed
grated rind and juice of ½ unwaxed lemon
1 tablespoon sumac

These spiced burgers are delicious served with flatbreads, salad leaves and large spoonfuls of sumac yogurt dip.

Using a spiralizer fitted with a 3 mm (⅛ inch) spaghetti blade, spiralize the courgette.

Place all the burger ingredients in a large bowl and use your hands to mix the ingredients together. Divide the mixture into 6 portions and shape into large burgers. Transfer the burgers to a plate and chill in the refrigerator for 15 minutes.

Place the burgers on a nonstick baking sheet and brush the burgers with a little oil. Cook the burgers under a preheated hot grill for 6–7 minutes on each side or until cooked through.

While the burgers are cooking, make the dip. Place all the ingredients in a small bowl, mix together and season to taste.

Serve the burgers hot with the sumac yogurt dip alongside.

courgetti with sundried tomato pesto

Serves 4
Prepare in 10 minutes
Cook in 5 minutes

4 courgettes, ends trimmed and halved widthways
2 tablespoons olive oil
freshly ground black pepper
rocket leaves, to serve

For the sundried tomato pesto
1 x 280 g (9½ oz) jar sundried tomatoes in olive oil
50 g (2 oz) pine nuts, lightly toasted
2 garlic cloves, chopped
1 teaspoon sea salt flakes
50 g (2 oz) basil leaves
125 g (4 oz) Parmesan cheese, grated

This recipe makes more sundried tomato pesto than you will need: the leftover pesto can be stored for 3–4 days in a jar or airtight container in the refrigerator. If you prefer to eat the courgetti raw, just toss it in the pesto sauce and leave to stand for 10 minutes to absorb the flavours.

First, make the sundried tomato pesto. Drain the sundried tomatoes, reserving the oil, and place them in a food processor with the pine nuts, garlic and salt. Blitz to make a paste – you may need to scrape the mixture down the sides of the food processor with a rubber spatula from time to time. Add the basil leaves a few at a time and pulse until combined. Transfer to a bowl and stir in the Parmesan and the reserved oil.

Using a spiralizer fitted with a 3 mm (⅛ inch) spaghetti blade, spiralize the courgettes.

Heat the oil in a large frying pan and then gently sauté the courgettes over a medium heat for 2–3 minutes until heated through. Stir in half of the sundried tomato pesto and toss to coat the courgettes in the sauce.

Divide between 4 bowls, season with plenty of pepper and serve with rocket leaves.

herby sausage and bacon hash

Serves 2
Prepare in 5 minutes
Cook in 15–20 minutes

2 Cumberland or herby sausages
1 onion, ends trimmed
2 large potatoes, about 450 g (14½ oz) peeled, ends trimmed and halved widthways
1 tablespoon sunflower oil
2 smoked back bacon rashers, chopped
2 large eggs
salt and freshly ground black pepper

Squeeze the sausagemeat out of the sausage skins and break it into small pieces.

Using a spiralizer fitted with a 3 mm (⅛ inch) spaghetti blade, spiralize the onion and potatoes, keeping them separate. Place the spiralized potatoes on a clean tea towel or kitchen paper and gently squeeze out any excess liquid.

Heat the oil in a frying pan, add the sausagemeat and bacon and cook over a medium heat for 3–4 minutes, stirring with a wooden spoon to break up the sausagemeat, until the sausagemeat is brown and crispy. Add the spiralized onion and cook for 2 minutes or until softened, then stir in the potatoes and season with salt and pepper. Mix well and cook for 3–4 minutes, until starting to crisp. Turn over the mixture and cook for a further 3–4 minutes, until the potatoes are crispy and cooked through.

Using the back of a spoon, make 2 holes in the mixture. Crack in the eggs and cook for 2–3 minutes or until the eggs are just set. Serve immediately.

plantain, chicken and coconut curry

Serves 4
Prepare in 10 minutes
Cook in 30 minutes

2 green plantains (the straightest ones you can find)
1 onion, ends trimmed
2 tablespoons groundnut oil
1 garlic clove, crushed
2.5 cm (1 inch) piece fresh root ginger, grated
1 tablespoon medium curry powder
3 boneless, skinless chicken breasts, cut into chunks
400 ml (14 fl oz) coconut milk
300 ml (½ pint) chicken stock
finely grated rind and juice of 2 unwaxed limes
200 g (7 oz) baby spinach
salt and freshly ground black pepper

To serve
naan breads
2 limes, halved

Cut the plantains in half widthways. Score the outside of the skins and peel off, then trim the ends. Using a spiralizer fitted with a 3 mm (⅛ inch) spaghetti blade, spiralize the plantains. Spiralize the onion and keep separate from the plantain.

Heat 1 tablespoon of the oil in a large saucepan, add the spiralized onion, garlic and ginger and cook gently over a medium heat for 3–4 minutes, until softened. Add the curry powder and cook for 1 minute, then stir in the chicken and cook for 3–4 minutes, until lightly browned. Stir in the coconut milk and stock, bring to the boil and then cover and simmer for 15 minutes. Season to taste with salt and pepper. Stir in most of the spiralized plantain, reserving a handful to fry later. Cover the pan and simmer for 5–6 minutes, until just tender. Remove the saucepan from the heat. Stir in the lime rind and juice and the baby spinach, cover and leave to stand for 2–3 minutes, until the spinach is wilted.

Meanwhile, heat the remaining oil in a small frying pan and cook the reserved spiralized plantain over a medium heat for 2–3 minutes, until crisp.

Spoon the curry into bowls and sprinkle with the crispy plantain. Serve immediately with naan bread and lime halves to squeeze over.

pork, apple and sage patties

Serves 4
Prepare in 5 minutes
Cook in 15 minutes

1 small onion, ends trimmed
1 large eating apple, ends trimmed
500 g (1 lb) lean minced pork
2 tablespoons chopped sage
1 tablespoon wholegrain mustard
25 g (1 oz) dried breadcrumbs
1 tablespoon sunflower oil
200 ml (7 fl oz) hot chicken stock
salt and freshly ground black pepper
seasonal vegetables, to serve

These pork patties also makes excellent burgers – just brush them with a little oil and then grill for 6–7 minutes on each side or until cooked through.

Using a spiralizer fitted with a 3 mm (⅛ inch) spaghetti blade, spiralize the onion and apple.

Place the minced pork, spiralized onion and apple, sage, mustard and breadcrumbs in a large bowl and season with salt and pepper. Mix well, using your hand, until all the ingredients are combined. Divide the mixture into 12 portions and shape into patties.

Heat the oil in a large frying pan and then cook the patties over a medium heat for 3–4 minutes on each side, until cooked through. Remove the patties from the pan and set aside.

Pour the stock into the frying pan, bring to a simmer and cook for 2 minutes, stirring and scraping the base of the pan, until the liquid has reduced slightly.

Divide the patties between 4 plates and serve them with seasonal vegetables and the pan juices.

courgette-crust Margherita pizza

Serves 4
Prepare in 10 minutes
Cook in 30 minutes

a little sunflower oil, for brushing
4 courgettes, ends trimmed and halved widthways
1 teaspoon garlic paste
125 g (4 oz) reduced-fat mature Cheddar cheese
2 teaspoons dried mixed herbs
50 g (2 oz) gluten-free plain flour
2 eggs, beaten
1 teaspoon salt

For the tomato sauce
1 x 200 g (7 oz) can chopped tomatoes
2 tablespoons tomato purée
½ teaspoon caster sugar
1 teaspoon dried mixed herbs

For the toppings
200 g (7 oz) mozzarella cheese, sliced
2 tomatoes, sliced
2 tablespoons pesto
a few basil leaves

This pizza is suitable for those on a gluten-free diet. You can adapt the recipe by adding any of your favourite toppings.

Line a large baking sheet with nonstick baking paper and brush with a little oil.

Using a spiralizer fitted with a 3 mm (⅛ inch) spaghetti blade, spiralize the courgettes. Place the spiralized courgettes on a clean tea towel or kitchen paper and gently squeeze out any excess liquid.

Transfer the courgettes to a large bowl, add the garlic paste, Cheddar, mixed herbs, flour, eggs and salt and mix well. Tip the mixture into the centre of the prepared baking sheet and pat into a 30 cm (12 inch) round – this courgette crust will form the base of the pizza.

Bake in a preheated oven, 200°C (400°F), Gas Mark 6, for 20 minutes or until golden brown. Place a separate large baking sheet on top of the courgette crust and carefully invert onto the new baking sheet. Peel off the baking paper and return the courgette crust to the oven for a further 5 minutes, until golden.

Meanwhile, place all the tomato sauce ingredients in a small saucepan and simmer over a low heat for 5 minutes, stirring occasionally. Allow the sauce to cool.

Spread the tomato sauce over the courgette crust, arrange the mozzarella and tomatoes over the top and drizzle with the pesto. Return to the oven and bake for 5–6 minutes or until the cheese has melted. Scatter over the basil leaves and serve immediately.

Mexican spicy bean burgers

Serves 4
Prepare in 15 minutes, plus chilling
Cook in 15–20 minutes

1 onion, ends trimmed
1 sweet potato, about 275 g (9 oz), peeled, ends trimmed and halved widthways
1 tablespoon sunflower oil
1 green chilli, deseeded and finely chopped
2 teaspoons Mexican or fajita spice mix
1 x 400 g (13 oz) can red kidney beans, drained and rinsed
4 tablespoons chopped fresh coriander
1 egg
2 teaspoons chipotle paste
salt and freshly ground black pepper

To serve
4 flour tortillas
crisp green lettuce
fresh tomato salsa
guacamole
4 lime wedges

Using a spiralizer fitted with a 3 mm (⅛ inch) spaghetti blade, spiralize the onion and sweet potato.

Heat the oil in a small frying pan and cook the spiralized onion and chilli over a medium heat for 2–3 minutes, until softened. Stir in the spice mix and cook for 1 minute. Add the spiralized sweet potato and stir-fry for 4–5 minutes, until softened. Leave to cool slightly.

Mash the kidney beans in a large bowl with a potato masher or fork, then add the coriander and season well with salt and pepper. Stir in the sweet potato mixture.

In a small bowl, beat together the egg with the chipotle paste. Pour over the sweet potato and bean mixture and mix well with a fork. Divide the mixture into 4 portions and shape into burgers, using your hands. Transfer the burgers to a plate and chill in the refrigerator for 15 minutes.

Place the burgers on a nonstick baking sheet and cook under a preheated medium-hot grill for 4–5 minutes on each side, until golden and cooked through.

Warm the tortillas. Top each tortilla with some lettuce, a spoonful of salsa and a burger and finish with a spoonful of guacamole. Serve with lime wedges to squeeze over.

beef and broccoli stir-fry

Serves 4
Prepare in 10 minutes, plus marinating
Cook in 10 minutes

2.5 cm (1 inch) piece fresh root ginger, peeled and cut into thin strips
1 garlic clove, crushed
1 teaspoon cornflour
2 tablespoons dark soy sauce
2 tablespoons sherry or Chinese cooking wine (Shaoxing)
500 g (1 lb) beef rump steak, trimmed of fat and cut into thin strips
2 carrots, peeled, ends trimmed and halved widthways
1 head of broccoli, about 200 g (7 oz)
1 tablespoon sunflower oil
75 g (3 oz) cashew nuts, toasted
300 g (10 oz) cooked egg noodles
2 tablespoons oyster sauce
100 ml (3½ fl oz) beef stock or water

Don't throw away broccoli stalks: spiralize them and add them to stir-fries instead.

In a large bowl, mix together the ginger, garlic, cornflour and 1 tablespoon each of soy sauce and sherry or Chinese cooking wine. Stir in the beef and leave to marinate for 15 minutes.

Using a spiralizer fitted with a 3 mm (⅛ inch) spaghetti blade, spiralize the carrots. Change to a 6 mm (¼ inch) flat noodle blade, cut the broccoli stalk away from the florets and spiralize the stalk. Break the rest of the broccoli into small florets.

Bring a large saucepan of water to the boil and cook the broccoli florets for 2 minutes. Drain and plunge into cold water to stop the cooking. Drain again and pat dry with kitchen paper.

Heat 2 teaspoons of the oil in a wok or large frying pan over a high heat until really hot. Add the beef strips and marinade and stir-fry for 2–3 minutes, until the beef has browned. Remove the beef from the pan with a slotted spoon, transfer to a plate and set aside.

Add the remaining oil to the wok or frying pan. When the oil is hot, add the carrots, spiralized broccoli stalk, broccoli florets and cashew nuts and cook for 2–3 minutes, until the vegetables are just tender.

Return the beef and any meat juices to the wok or frying pan. Add the noodles and stir in the remaining soy sauce and sherry or Chinese cooking wine, oyster sauce and stock or water. Cook, stirring constantly, until the sauce has coated all the ingredients. Serve immediately.

smoked haddock fishcakes

Serves 4
Prepare in 20 minutes
Cook in 30–35 minutes

250 g (8 oz) skinless and boneless smoked haddock fillets
2 potatoes, about 450 g (14½ oz), peeled and ends trimmed
2 tablespoons chopped parsley
2 tablespoons light mayonnaise
1 tablespoon wholegrain mustard
2 tablespoons plain flour
1 egg, beaten
salt and freshly ground black pepper

To serve
rocket leaves
lemon wedges

Poach the smoked haddock in a saucepan of simmering water for 4–5 minutes or until the fish flakes easily. Remove the fish with a slotted spoon, transfer to a plate and leave to cool.

Using a spiralizer fitted with a 3 mm (⅛ inch) spaghetti blade, spiralize the potatoes. Place the spiralized potatoes in a saucepan of boiling water and simmer for 3–4 minutes, until just tender. Drain and allow to cool slightly.

Flake the fish into a large bowl. Add the potatoes, parsley, mayonnaise, mustard, flour and egg, mix well and season with salt and pepper.

Line a large baking sheet with nonstick baking paper. Place an 8.5 cm (3½ inch) metal ring or cutter on the baking sheet and fill the ring or cutter with some of the fish mixture to form a thick cake. Remove the ring or cutter and repeat 7 more times to make 8 fishcakes in total.

Bake the fishcakes in a preheated oven, 200° (400°), Gas Mark 6, for 20–25 minutes, until crispy. Serve the fishcakes with rocket leaves and lemon wedges to squeeze over.

sides and extras

sweet potato dauphinoise

Serves 6
Prepare in 10 minutes
Cook in 1 hour

15 g (½ oz) butter
500 g (1 lb) potatoes, peeled, ends trimmed and halved widthways
500 g (1 lb) sweet potatoes, peeled, ends trimmed and halved widthways
1 large onion, ends trimmed
2 garlic cloves, crushed
2 tablespoons chopped rosemary
450 ml (¾ pint) semi-skimmed milk
300 ml (½ pint) half-fat crème fraîche
salt and freshly ground black pepper

Using a little of the butter, lightly grease a 1.5 litre (2½ pint) ovenproof dish. Using a spiralizer fitted with a ribbon blade, spiralize the potatoes and sweet potatoes, keeping them separate. Change to a 3 mm (⅛ inch) spaghetti blade and spiralize the onion.

Melt the remaining butter in a large saucepan over a medium heat. Add the spiralized onion and cook for 3–4 minutes, until softened. Stir in the garlic and rosemary and cook for 1 minute. Stir in the milk and crème fraîche, season with salt and pepper and then stir in the spiralized potatoes. Bring to a simmer, then cover and cook over a low heat for 5 minutes. Stir in the spiralized sweet potatoes, cover and simmer for 3 minutes.

Transfer the mixture to the prepared dish, cover with foil and bake in a preheated oven, 160°C (325°F), Gas Mark 3, for 30 minutes. Uncover and cook for a further 10 minutes or until the potatoes are tender.

spicy Asian coleslaw

Serves 4–6
Prepare in 10 minutes

1 cucumber, ends trimmed and cut into 3 pieces widthways
1 large carrot, peeled, ends trimmed and cut into 3 pieces widthways
1 mooli, about 250 g (8 oz), peeled, ends trimmed and halved widthways
4 tablespoons chopped fresh coriander
2 tablespoons sesame seeds, lightly toasted

For the dressing
finely grated rind and juice of 2 unwaxed limes
1 tablespoon rice wine vinegar
2 teaspoons grated fresh root ginger
1 small red chilli, deseeded and chopped
1 teaspoon palm or soft brown sugar
1 teaspoon sesame oil

Using a spiralizer fitted with a 3 mm (⅛ inch) spaghetti blade, spiralize the cucumber and pat dry with kitchen paper. Using the same blade, spiralize the carrot and mooli.

To make the dressing, in a small bowl, mix together the lime rind and juice, vinegar, ginger, chilli, sugar and sesame oil and stir until the sugar has dissolved.

Place the spiralized cucumber, carrot and mooli in a large bowl and sprinkle over the coriander and sesame seeds. Pour over the dressing and toss well to coat all the ingredients. Chill the coleslaw in the refrigerator until ready to serve.

spiralized root vegetable rosti

Serves 4
Prepare in 10 minutes
Cook in 30–40 minutes

300 g (10 oz) floury potatoes, such as King Edward, peeled and ends trimmed
150 g (5 oz) carrots, peeled, ends trimmed and halved widthways
150 g (5 oz) parsnips, peeled, ends trimmed and halved widthways
1 onion, ends trimmed
1 tablespoon sunflower oil
2 teaspoons chopped thyme leaves
salt and freshly ground black pepper

This is a great way of using up any odd root vegetables that are left in the refrigerator. A rosti is a great accompaniment for roast meats or you can turn it into a main meal by serving it with poached eggs.

Using a spiralizer fitted with a 3 mm (⅛ inch) spaghetti blade, spiralize all the vegetables, keeping the onion separate.

Place the spiralized potatoes, carrots and parsnips in a steamer over a pan of boiling water and steam for 5 minutes or until the potatoes are sticky and the carrots and parsnip are just tender.

Meanwhile, heat the oil in a 23 cm (9 inch) nonstick frying pan and cook the spiralized onion over a medium heat for 2–3 minutes, until softened.

Stir in the steamed vegetables and thyme and season with salt and pepper. Cook for 4–5 minutes, without stirring, until the bottom of the vegetables starts to crisp. Turn over the vegetables, pat down and continue to cook for a further 4–5 minutes. Repeat this process 2 more times or until the rosti is crispy and cooked through. Cut the rosti into wedges and serve.

mustardy celeriac and potato gratin

Serves 6
Prepare in 10 minutes
Cook in 1 hour

500 g (1 lb) floury potatoes, such as King Edward, peeled and ends trimmed
400 g (13 oz) celeriac, peeled and cut into 12 cm (5 inch) chunks
3 garlic cloves, crushed
300 ml (½ pint) double cream
300 ml (½ pint) milk
2 tablespoons wholegrain mustard
knob of butter, plus extra for greasing
salt and freshly ground black pepper

Grease a shallow 1.5 litre (2½ pint) ovenproof dish. Using a spiralizer fitted with a 6 mm (¼ inch) flat noodle blade, spiralize the potatoes and celeriac, keeping them separate.

Place a handful of the spiralized potatoes in the base of the prepared dish, sprinkle over a little of the garlic and season with salt and pepper. Repeat, alternating layers of spiralized celeriac and potato, until the dish is full.

Whisk the cream, milk and mustard together in a bowl and then pour over the vegetables. Dot the surface of the gratin with butter and bake in a preheated oven, 160°C (325°F), Gas Mark 3, for 1 hour, stirring halfway through the cooking time, until golden and tender.

crispy potato fries with rosemary and garlic

Serves 2–3
Prepare in 5 minutes
Cook in 10 minutes

2 large potatoes, peeled, ends trimmed and halved widthways
1 litre (1¾ pints) vegetable or sunflower oil, for deep frying
4 rosemary sprigs
8 garlic cloves, unpeeled
sea salt flakes, for sprinkling

Using a spiralizer fitted with a 6 mm (¼ inch) flat noodle blade, spiralize the potatoes.

Heat the vegetable or sunflower oil in a wok or deep, heavy-based saucepan to 180–190°C (350–375°F), or until a cube of bread dropped into the oil turns golden brown in 30 seconds. Alternatively, you can use a deep-fat fryer.

Drop the rosemary and garlic into the hot oil and cook for 1 minute. Add the spiralized potatoes and deep-fry for 6–8 minutes, until golden brown and crispy. Remove from the oil with a slotted spoon and drain on kitchen paper. Sprinkle the fries with sea salt and serve immediately.

cucumber and mint raita

Serves 4
Prepare in 5 minutes

½ cucumber, ends trimmed and halved widthways
200 ml (7 fl oz) natural yogurt
2 tablespoons chopped mint
½ teaspoon salt
½ teaspoon ground cumin

This cooling raita is really quick to make. It is the perfect accompaniment for spicy dishes such as Crispy Onion Bhajis (see page 24).

Using a spiralizer fitted with a 3 mm (⅛ inch) spaghetti blade, spiralize the cucumber. Dry the spiralized cucumber on kitchen paper.

Place the cucumber in a large bowl and mix together with all the remaining ingredients. Chill in the refrigerator until ready to serve.

beetroot, potato and chive rosti

Serves 4
Prepare in 10 minutes
Cook in 20 minutes

150 g (5 oz) floury potatoes, such as King Edward, peeled and ends trimmed
200 g (7 oz) fresh beetroot, scrubbed and ends trimmed
2 tablespoons chopped chives
2 tablespoons olive oil
salt and freshly ground black pepper

Using a spiralizer fitted with a 3 mm (⅛ inch) spaghetti blade, spiralize the potatoes and beetroot. Place the spiralized vegetables on a clean tea towel or kitchen paper and gently squeeze out any excess liquid.

Put the vegetables in a bowl, lightly season with salt and pepper, add the chives and drizzle with the oil. Using your hands, mix the vegetables to coat them with the oil, herbs and seasoning.

Place an 8.5 cm (3½ inch) metal ring or cutter on a large nonstick baking sheet and press a little of the rosti mixture into the ring or cutter to form a thin cake. Remove the ring or cutter and repeat 7 more times to make 8 rosti in total. (Alternatively, you can shape the rosti with your hands.)

Bake the rosti in a preheated oven, 200°C (400°F), Gas Mark 6, for 15 minutes, until crisp and golden. Carefully flip over the rosti and cook for a further 5 minutes, until crisp.

Bramley apple and Calvados sauce

Serves 4
Prepare in 5 minutes
Cook in 10 minutes

3 Bramley apples, about 750 g (1½ lb), peeled and ends trimmed
finely grated rind of ½ unwaxed lemon
25 g (1 oz) caster sugar
25 g (1 oz) butter
2 tablespoons Calvados

This apple sauce is really easy to make and is delicious served with roast pork or goose. It will keep for about 1 week in the refrigerator and also freezes well.

Using a spiralizer fitted with a 6 mm (¼ inch) flat noodle blade, spiralize the apples.

Place the spiralized apples in a saucepan with the remaining ingredients and mix well. Cover and cook over a gentle heat for 8–10 minutes, stirring occasionally, until the apples are soft. Allow the sauce to cool.

spicy potato curls

Serves 4
Prepare in 5 minutes
Cook in 20 minutes

450 g (14½ oz) potatoes, peeled and ends trimmed
2 tablespoons sunflower oil
1 teaspoon garlic salt
2 teaspoons smoked paprika
1 teaspoon dried mixed herbs
salt and freshly ground black pepper

Line a large baking sheet with nonstick baking paper. Using a spiralizer fitted with a 6 mm (¼ inch) flat noodle blade, spiralize the potatoes.

Place the spiralized potatoes in a large bowl, add all the remaining ingredients and mix well to evenly coat the potatoes. Spread out the spiralized potatoes in a single layer on the prepared baking sheet.

Bake in a preheated oven, 200°C (400°F), Gas Mark 6, for 10 minutes, then stir the potato curls, moving the outside crispy ones to the centre, and bake for a further 10 minutes, until golden and crispy. Serve immediately.

celeriac remoulade

Serves 4
Prepare in 10 minutes, plus standing

juice of 1 lemon
4 heaped tablespoons light mayonnaise
2 tablespoons half-fat crème fraîche or fromage frais
2 tablespoons Dijon mustard
2 tablespoons chopped parsley
1 small celeriac, about 500 g (1 lb)
salt and freshly ground black pepper

This creamy dish is the perfect accompaniment for cold meats or smoked fish. The remoulade can be stored in the refrigerator for up to 2 days.

In a large bowl, mix together the lemon juice, mayonnaise, crème fraîche or fromage frais, mustard and parsley and season to taste with salt and pepper.

Using a sharp knife, remove the knobbly bits from the celeriac. Peel the celeriac, cut it in half widthways and trim to make the ends flat. Using a spiralizer fitted with a 3 mm (⅛ inch) spaghetti blade, spiralize the celeriac.

Immediately stir the spiralized celeriac into the creamy mixture, until evenly coated, and leave to stand for 30 minutes before serving.

spicy cucumber pickle

Serves 4
Prepare in 10 minutes, plus marinating

- 1 cucumber, ends trimmed and cut into 4 pieces widthways
- 2 teaspoons salt
- 4 tablespoons rice wine vinegar
- 3 tablespoons caster sugar
- 1 small red chilli, deseeded and finely chopped
- 2.5 cm (1 inch) piece fresh root ginger, peeled and grated

This pretty cucumber pickle is delicious served with seared salmon or chicken. Keep any leftover pickle in the refrigerator and use within a couple of days while the cucumber retains it crunch.

Using a spiralizer fitted with a ribbon blade, spiralize the cucumber. Dry the spiralized cucumber on kitchen paper and then place it in a large bowl.

Whisk together all the remaining ingredients in a small bowl and then pour over the cucumber. Gently toss to coat the cucumber, cover and leave to marinate for at least 1 hour or overnight in the refrigerator. To serve, drain the pickle from the marinade.

Moroccan carrot salad

Serves 4
Prepare in 10 minutes, plus marinating

450 g (14½ oz) large carrots, peeled and halved widthways
2 tablespoons orange juice
1 tablespoon lemon juice
2 teaspoons orange blossom water
2 tablespoons extra virgin olive oil
½ teaspoon ground cumin
½ teaspoon ground cinnamon
1 teaspoon icing sugar
1 preserved lemon, cut in half, pith and pulp removed and skin finely chopped
2 tablespoons chopped mint
sea salt flakes and freshly ground black pepper
handful of mint leaves, to garnish

Carrots are usually grated for a Moroccan carrot salad but spiralizing them saves time and also gives the carrots a lovely crunchy texture.

Using a spiralizer fitted with a 6 mm (¼ inch) flat noodle blade or a ribbon blade, spiralize the carrots.

Combine the orange juice, lemon juice, orange blossom water, olive oil, cumin, cinnamon and icing sugar in a bowl and whisk together. Season to taste with salt and pepper.

Add the spiralized carrots, preserved lemon and mint and lightly toss. Place in the refrigerator and leave to marinate for 1–2 hours. Garnish with the mint leaves just before serving.

roasted beetroot with balsamic glaze

Serves 4
Prepare in 5 minutes
Cook in 15–20 minutes

- 4 fresh beetroot, scrubbed and ends trimmed
- 1 tablespoon olive oil
- 3 tablespoons balsamic vinegar
- sea salt flakes and freshly ground black pepper

Roasted beetroot with balsamic vinegar is a perfect combination of flavours. This is great served as an accompaniment for meat or used in salads.

Using a spiralizer fitted with a 6 mm (¼ inch) flat noodle blade, spiralize the beetroot.

Place the spiralized beetroot in a roasting tin, drizzle over the oil and 2 tablespoons of the vinegar and season well with salt and pepper. Mix well.

Roast the beetroot in a preheated oven, 190°C (375° F), Gas Mark 5, for 15–20 minutes, turning halfway through the cooking time, until tender and slightly crispy. Stir in the remaining vinegar and allow to cool.

steamed vegetables with honey

Serves 4
Prepare in 5 minutes
Cook in 5 minutes

2 large carrots, peeled, ends trimmed and halved widthways
3 courgettes, ends trimmed and halved widthways
1 tablespoon honey
1 tablespoon lemon juice
½ teaspoon caraway seeds (optional)
salt and freshly ground black pepper

Using a spiralizer fitted with a ribbon blade, spiralize the carrots and courgettes.

In a small bowl, mix together the honey, lemon juice and caraway seeds, if using.

Place the spiralized carrots in a steamer over a pan of boiling water and steam for 2 minutes. Add the spiralized courgettes and steam for a further 3 minutes or until the vegetables are just tender.

Transfer the steamed vegetables to a serving bowl, pour over the honey mixture and toss well. Season to taste with salt and pepper and serve immediately.

spiced swede and pea fritters

Makes 12
Prepare in 10 minutes
Cook in 15–20 minutes

1 small swede, about 625 g (1¼ lb), peeled and cut into 12 cm (5 inch) chunks
75 g (3 oz) gram flour
½ teaspoon ground turmeric
2 teaspoons garam masala
1 teaspoon cumin seeds
1 green chilli, deseeded and finely chopped
1 egg, beaten
100 ml (3½ fl oz) milk
1 teaspoon garlic paste
1 teaspoon ginger paste
2 tablespoons chopped fresh coriander
100 g (3½ oz) frozen peas, defrosted
1 tablespoon groundnut or sunflower oil, for frying
salt and freshly ground black pepper

These spicy fritters are perfect for serving with grilled tandoori chicken or fish. They also make a great starter served with some Cucumber and Mint Raita (see page 92) or mango chutney.

Using a spiralizer fitted with a 3 mm (⅛ inch) spaghetti blade, spiralize the swede. Place the spiralized swede in a steamer over a pan of simmering water and steam for 4 minutes, until just tender. Allow to cool slightly.

Meanwhile, in a large bowl, mix together the flour, spices and chilli. Whisk together the egg, milk and garlic and ginger pastes in a small jug. Pour the egg mixture into the flour mixture and stir to make a thick batter. Stir in the coriander and peas, season with salt and pepper and then stir in the swede.

Heat a little oil in a large nonstick frying pan over a medium heat. Cooking 4 fritters at a time, add heaped tablespoons of the batter to the pan, flatten slightly and cook for 2–3 minutes on each side, until crisp and brown. Repeat until all the batter is used up. Serve immediately.

crispy Parmesan and onion spirals

Serves 2–3
Prepare in 10 minutes
Cook in 10 minutes

2 large onions, ends trimmed
2–3 tablespoons plain flour
2 eggs
100 g (3½ oz) panko breadcrumbs
50 g (2 oz) Parmesan cheese, grated
1 litre (1¾ pints) vegetable or sunflower oil, for deep frying
salt and freshly ground black pepper

Using a spiralizer fitted with a 6 mm (¼ inch) flat noodle blade, spiralize the onions.

Sprinkle the flour onto a plate. Beat the eggs together in a bowl. Mix together the breadcrumbs and Parmesan in a separate bowl and season with salt and pepper.

Place the spiralized onions in the flour, toss to lightly coat and dust off any excess. Dip the onions in the egg mixture and then roll them in the Parmesan crumbs to coat.

Heat the vegetable or sunflower oil in a wok or deep, heavy-based saucepan to 180–190°C (350–375°F), or until a cube of bread dropped into the oil turns golden brown in 30 seconds. Alternatively, you can use a deep-fat fryer.

Carefully drop tablespoonfuls of the onion mixture into the hot oil, cooking about 4 at a time, and deep-fry the spirals for 2–3 minutes, until golden and crispy. Remove from the oil with a slotted spoon, drain on kitchen paper and keep warm while you cook the remaining mixture. Serve immediately.

sweet treats

apple frangipane tart

Serves 8
Prepare in 15 minutes
Cook in 1 hour

350 g (11½ oz) ready-made shortcrust pastry
100 g (3½ oz) unsalted butter
100 g (3½ oz) caster sugar
2 large eggs
200 g (7 oz) ground almonds
½ teaspoon almond extract
1 tablespoon plain flour, plus extra for dusting
2 large red eating apples, ends trimmed
25 g (1 oz) flaked almonds
2 tablespoons apricot conserve or jam
whipped or double cream, to serve

On a lightly floured surface, roll out the pastry until large enough to fit a 25 cm (10 inch) loose-bottomed tart tin. Line the tin with the pastry. Prick the base with a fork, cover with nonstick baking paper and fill with baking beans. Place the tin on a baking sheet and bake in a preheated oven, 190°C (375°F), Gas Mark 5, for 15 minutes. Remove the baking beans and paper and return to the oven for 5 minutes, until golden.

In a large bowl, cream together the butter and sugar until light and fluffy. Gradually beat in the eggs and then stir in the ground almonds, almond extract and flour. Spoon the mixture into the pastry case.

Using a spiralizer fitted with a 6 mm (¼ inch) flat noodle blade, spiralize the apples.

Arrange the spiralized apples on top of the tart and sprinkle over the flaked almonds. Bake in a preheated oven, 180°C (350°F), Gas Mark 4, for 40–45 minutes, until golden and set.

Warm the apricot conserve or jam in a small saucepan and then brush over the top of the tart. Serve slices of the tart with spoonfuls of whipped or double cream.

beetroot and chocolate brownies

Makes about 24
Prepare in 15 minutes
Cook in 40 minutes

275 g (9 oz) fresh beetroot, scrubbed and ends trimmed
250 g (8 oz) dark chocolate, broken into pieces (or use dark chocolate drops)
250 g (8 oz) butter, plus extra for greasing
3 eggs
275g (9 oz) golden caster sugar
1 teaspoon vanilla extract
75 g (3 oz) plain flour
50 g (2 oz) cocoa powder
pinch of salt

Grease the base of a 20 cm (8 inch) square cake tin and line with nonstick baking paper. Using a spiralizer fitted with a 3 mm (⅛ inch) spaghetti blade, spiralize the beetroot.

Place the spiralized beetroot in a saucepan and cover with cold water. Bring to the boil, then reduce the heat, cover and simmer for about 8 minutes or until tender. Drain well.

Place the beetroot in a food processor and whiz for a few minutes to form a smooth purée. Set aside.

Place the chocolate and butter in a heatproof bowl set over a saucepan of simmering water, taking care that the bowl does not actually touch the water. Leave until just melted, stirring occasionally, then remove from the heat and set aside.

In a large mixing bowl, whisk together the eggs, sugar and vanilla extract until pale and fluffy. Beat in the puréed beetroot and melted chocolate. Sift in the flour, cocoa powder and salt and then fold them in until fully combined. Tip the batter into the prepared baking tin, smoothing the top with a palette knife or spatula.

Bake in a preheated oven, 180°C (350°F), Gas Mark 4, for 30 minutes or until the centre is almost set but still wobbles when you gently shake the tin. Remove from the oven and allow the cake to cool completely before carefully removing it from the tin. Peel off the baking paper and cut the cake into squares.

Asian pear fruit salad

Serves 4
Prepare in 5 minutes, plus cooling
Cook in 10 minutes

100 g (3½ oz) golden caster sugar
2 lemon grass stalks, bruised and roughly chopped
2.5 cm (1 inch) piece fresh root ginger, peeled and finely sliced
150 ml (¼ pint) cold water
4 firm Asian pears (you can use normal pears or apples if you can't find Asian pears), ends trimmed
2 tablespoons chopped mint
100 g (3½ oz) pomegranate seeds
4 tablespoons fresh or dried coconut shavings or desiccated coconut

Place the sugar, lemon grass, ginger and measurement water in a saucepan. Cook over a low heat, stirring occasionally, until the sugar has dissolved. Bring the syrup to the boil, then reduce the heat and simmer for 5 minutes. Remove from heat and allow to cool.

Once the syrup has cooled, use a spiralizer fitted with a ribbon blade to spiralize the pears – don't do this ahead of time or the pears will brown. Place the spiralized pears in a salad bowl.

Remove the lemon grass from the syrup and discard. Pour the syrup over the pears and then gently stir in the mint and pomegranate seeds. Chill in the refrigerator until ready to serve. To serve, divide the salad between 4 bowls and sprinkle over the coconut.

carrot cake muffins

Makes 12
Prepare in 10 minutes
Cook in 18–20 minutes

1½ carrots, about 175 g (6 oz), peeled, ends trimmed and the whole carrot halved widthways
175 g (6 oz) unsalted butter, softened
175 g (6 oz) caster sugar
grated rind of 1 unwaxed orange and 1 tablespoon orange juice
175 g (6 oz) self-raising flour
2 teaspoons ground mixed spice
2 large eggs
50 g (2 oz) walnut pieces, chopped

For the frosting
200 g (7 oz) low-fat cream cheese
2 tablespoons icing sugar
1 tablespoon orange juice
2 teaspoons grated orange rind

The spiralized carrots make these muffins deliciously moist. They are decorated with an orange and cream cheese frosting and spiralized carrot curls.

Line a muffin tin with 12 paper muffin cases. Using a spiralizer fitted with a 3 mm (⅛ inch) spaghetti blade, spiralize the carrots.

Beat together the butter, sugar and orange rind in large bowl until pale and fluffy. Sift over the flour and mixed spice, then add the eggs and orange juice and whisk together until well combined. Stir in 125g (4 oz) spiralized carrots and the walnuts.

Divide the mixture between the muffin cases. Bake in a preheated oven, 180°C (350°F), Gas Mark 4, for 18–20 minutes, until risen and golden brown. Remove from the oven, place on a cooling rack and allow to cool.

To make the frosting, beat together all the ingredients in a bowl until smooth. Spoon the frosting into a piping bag fitted with a star-shaped nozzle and pipe the frosting onto the cooled muffins. (Alternatively, you can spread the frosting over the top of the muffins with a palette knife.) Decorate the muffins with the remaining carrot curls.

stem ginger and apple cookies

Makes 12–14
Prepare in 15 minutes
Cook in 8–10 minutes

125 g (4 oz) porridge oats
75 g (3 oz) sunflower seeds
125 g (4 oz) self-raising flour
150 g (5 oz) unsalted butter, cut into cubes
2 tablespoons apple juice
150 g (5 oz) soft light brown sugar
3 tablespoons of stem ginger syrup
1 large red eating apple, ends trimmed
3 pieces of stem ginger, chopped

Line 3 large baking sheets with nonstick baking paper.

Mix together the oats, sunflower seeds and flour in a large bowl.

Place the butter in a saucepan with the apple juice, sugar and ginger syrup and cook over a low heat, stirring with a wooden spoon, until the butter and sugar have melted.

Meanwhile, using a spiralizer fitted with a 3 mm (1/8 inch) spaghetti blade, spiralize the apple.

Pour the butter mixture over the dry ingredients and mix together until combined. Gently fold in the spiralized apple and stem ginger.

Place heaped dessertspoons of the mixture on each prepared baking sheet, leaving a fairly large space between each cookie to allow them to spread during cooking. Bake in a preheated oven, 160°C (325°F), Gas Mark 3, for 8–10 minutes, until golden. You may need to bake the cookies in batches.

Allow the cookies to cool on the baking sheets for a few minutes and then transfer them to a cooling rack with a palette knife. Leave them to cool until they become crisp.

autumn fruit salad

Serves 4
Prepare in 10 minutes, plus chilling

3 tablespoons maple syrup
½ teaspoon vanilla extract
1 teaspoon finely grated lemon rind
2 tablespoons lemon juice
¼ teaspoon ground cinnamon
2 firm pears, pointy ends trimmed
2 large red eating apples, ends trimmed
250 g (8 oz) blackberries
25 g (1 oz) pecan nuts, chopped

This colourful autumnal dessert combines juicy blackberries with crisp apples and pears. Ideally, this fruit salad should be eaten on the day it is prepared.

In a large bowl, whisk together the maple syrup, vanilla extract, lemon rind and juice and cinnamon.

Using a spiralizer fitted with a ribbon blade, spiralize the pears and apples.

Place the spiralized pears and apples in the bowl with the syrup mixture and toss to coat in the syrup mixture. Stir in the blackberries. Chill in the refrigerator for about 30 minutes to allow the flavours to mingle.

Divide the fruit salad between 4 bowls and sprinkle over the pecans.

pear tarte tatin

Serves 4–6
Prepare in 10 minutes
Cook in 40 minutes

3 large firm pears, pointy ends trimmed
125 g (4 oz) caster sugar
40 g (1½ oz) cold butter, cubed
½ teaspoon ground ginger
flour, for dusting
375 g (12 oz) ready-made, all-butter puff pastry
double cream, to serve

You need to use firm pears for this recipe, otherwise the pears will release too much juice and make the pastry soggy.

Using a spiralizer fitted with a 6 mm (¼ inch) flat noodle blade, spiralize the pears.

Place a 21 cm (8½ inch) ovenproof frying pan over a medium heat. Add the sugar and heat for 4–5 minutes, stirring constantly, until the sugar is a caramel colour. Add the butter and ginger and stir to combine.

Place the spiralized pears in the caramel and spoon over the mixture until the pears are coated. Turn the heat down and cook for 4–5 minutes, until slightly softened. Remove from the heat and leave to cool slightly.

On a lightly floured surface, roll out the pastry to about 5 mm (¼ inch) thick. Cut a disc slightly bigger than your frying pan (about 24 cm/9½ inches in diameter). Place the pastry disc on top of the pears and then carefully tuck the pastry snugly around the outside of the pears and down into the sides of the pan.

Bake the tart in a preheated oven, 200°C (400°F), Gas Mark 6, for 30 minutes or until the pastry is golden brown and puffed up. Remove from the oven and leave to stand for 10 minutes.

Loosen the edges with a knife, place a large serving plate over the top and carefully invert the pan to turn the tart onto the plate. Serve with double cream.

apple, raspberry and almond crumbles

Serves 4
Prepare in 10 minutes
Cook in 20–25 minutes

2 large or 3 medium red eating apples, ends trimmed
200 g (7 oz) fresh raspberries
2 tablespoons caster sugar
4 tablespoons apple juice
custard or vanilla ice cream, to serve

For the topping
125 g (4 oz) plain flour
75 g (3 oz) butter
4 tablespoons caster sugar
4 tablespoons ground almonds

This apple and raspberry dessert is topped with a delicious crunchy almond-flavoured crumble.

Using a spiralizer fitted with a 6 mm (¼ inch) flat noodle blade, spiralize the apples.

Place the spiralized apples in a large bowl and gently mix together with the raspberries and sugar. Divide the mixture between 4 x 250 ml (8 fl oz) ovenproof dishes and spoon 1 tablespoon of apple juice over the mixture in each dish.

Next, make the topping. In a large bowl, rub together the flour with the butter until the mixture resembles fine breadcrumbs (or use a food processor to do this). Stir in the sugar and almonds.

Sprinkle the topping over the apple and raspberry mixture, dividing the topping between the 4 dishes. Bake in a preheated oven, 190°C (375°F), Gas Mark 5, for 20–25 minutes, until golden and bubbling. Serve with custard or vanilla ice cream.

beetroot and blueberry pancakes

Serves 4
Prepare in 10 minutes
Cook in 10 minutes

1 fresh beetroot, scrubbed and ends trimmed
250 ml (8 fl oz) buttermilk
1 teaspoon vanilla extract
150 g (5 oz) buckwheat or plain flour
½ teaspoon salt
2 teaspoons baking powder
1 tablespoon caster sugar
1 egg
125 g (4 oz) fresh blueberries
1 tablespoon sunflower oil

To serve
0% Greek yogurt
handful of blueberries
maple syrup or honey

These pancakes sound unusual but the beetroot gives them a pretty pink colour and they have a slightly earthy taste that is tinged with bursts of sweet blueberries.

Using a spiralizer fitted with a 3 mm (⅛ inch) spaghetti blade, spiralize the beetroot.

Place the spiralized beetroot in a large jug with the buttermilk and vanilla extract. Blend with a stick blender to form a bright-red liquid.

Sift the flour, salt and baking powder into a large bowl and stir in the sugar. Add the egg and then gradually beat the beetroot mixture into the flour to make a smooth batter. Stir in the blueberries.

Heat a large nonstick frying pan over a medium heat. Dip a scrunched up piece of kitchen paper into the oil and carefully use this to grease the hot pan. Drop 4 large tablespoons of the batter into the pan (this will make 4 small pancakes) and cook for 2–3 minutes, until bubbles start to appear on the surface and the underside is golden brown. Flip over the pancakes and cook for a further 2 minutes. Keep the pancakes warm while you cook the remaining batter, greasing the pan with a little more oil if necesssary.

Place 2 pancakes on each plate and serve with a dollop of yogurt, some blueberries and a drizzle of maple syrup or honey.

apple, cinnamon and sultana muffins

Makes 10
Prepare in 10 minutes
Cook in 20–25 minutes

2 red eating apples, ends trimmed
275 g (9 oz) plain flour
1 tablespoon baking powder
½ teaspoon salt
1 teaspoon ground cinnamon
125 g (4 oz) caster sugar
1 large egg
150 ml (¼ pint) milk
75 ml (3 fl oz) sunflower oil
75 g (3 oz) sultanas
2 tablespoons soft brown sugar, for sprinkling

Line a muffin tin with 10 paper muffin cases. Using a spiralizer fitted with a 6 mm (¼ inch) flat noodle blade, spiralize the apples.

In a large bowl, sift together the flour, baking powder, salt, cinnamon and caster sugar.

In a jug, beat together the egg, milk and oil and pour over the dry ingredients. Mix until just combined and then stir in the spiralized apples and the sultanas.

Divide the mixture between the muffin cases and then sprinkle the tops with brown sugar. Bake in a preheated oven, 190°C (375°F), Gas Mark 5, for 20–25 minutes, until risen and firm. These muffins are delicious served both warm and cold.

salted caramel and pear pudding

Serves 4
Prepare in 15 minutes
Cook in 35–40 minutes

4 firm Conference pears, pointy ends trimmed
125 g (4 oz) plain flour
2 teaspoons baking powder
125 g (4 oz) caster sugar
200 ml (7 fl oz) milk
100 g (3½ oz) butter, melted, plus extra for greasing
1 egg, beaten
150 g (5 oz) light brown muscovado sugar
4 tablespoons golden syrup
2 teaspoon sea salt flakes
250 ml (8 fl oz) water
vanilla ice cream, to serve

This easy-to-make dessert combines juicy pears with a sticky salted caramel sauce and a light sponge. It is delicious served with vanilla ice cream.

Grease a 1.5 litre (2½ pint) ovenproof dish. Using a spiralizer fitted with a 6 mm (¼ inch) flat noodle blade, spiralize the pears. Place the spiralized pears in the base of the prepared dish.

Sift the flour and baking powder into a large bowl. Add the caster sugar, milk, melted butter and egg and whisk together for 2–3 minutes until well combined. Pour the mixture over the pears.

To make the salted caramel sauce, place the brown sugar, golden syrup and salt in a small saucepan and add the measurement water. Cook over a moderate heat, stirring until the sugar has dissolved, then bring to the boil.

Carefully pour the sauce over the pudding and bake in a preheated oven, 180°C (350°F), Gas Mark 4, for 30–35 minutes, until the sponge is set. Allow the pudding to stand for 5 minutes before serving with vanilla ice cream.

courgette and lemon drizzle cake

Serves 8
Prepare in 20 minutes
Cook in 40–45 minutes

2 courgettes, ends trimmed and halved widthways
finely grated rind of 2 unwaxed lemons
200 g (7 oz) unsalted butter, softened, plus extra for greasing
200 g (7 oz) caster sugar
3 eggs, beaten
200 g (7 oz) self-raising flour, sifted
a small handful of Candied Lemon Peel (see page 124), to decorate

For the lemon syrup
75 g (3 oz) granulated sugar
juice of 2 lemons (about 100 ml/ 3½ fl oz)

The spiralized courgettes add moisture to this really lemony cake. The cake's crusty topping is made by pouring lemon syrup over the top of the cake while it is still warm.

Grease a 20 cm (8 inch) springform cake tin and line the base with nonstick baking paper.

Using a spiralizer fitted with a 3mm (¼ inch) spaghetti blade, spiralize the courgettes. Roughly snip any really long spirals in half with scissors.

Place the lemon rind, butter and sugar in a mixing bowl and beat until light and fluffy. Add the eggs a little at a time, whisking well after each addition. If the mixture starts to curdle, add 1 tablespoon of the flour. Using a metal spoon, fold in the spiralized courgettes and flour until you have a really thick mixture.

Spoon the mixture into the prepared tin and bake in the centre of a preheated oven, 180°C (350°F), Gas Mark 4, for 40–45 minutes, until risen, golden and shrinking away from the sides of the tin.

Meanwhile, as soon as the cake goes into the oven, make the lemon syrup. Put the sugar and lemon juice in a small bowl and leave in a warm place (next to the oven is ideal) while the cake bakes, stirring the mixture occasionally.

Remove the cake from the oven and prick all over the surface of the cake, about 20 times, with a cocktail stick. Slowly drizzle over the lemon syrup, waiting a few moments for the syrup to sink in before adding more. Leave the cake to cool in the tin for 10 minutes, then remove from the tin and transfer to a cooling rack. Decorate with the candied lemon peel.

candied lemon peel

Makes enough to decorate 2 large cakes
Prepare in 5 minutes, plus cooling
Cook in 10 minutes

4 large unwaxed lemons
100 g (3½ oz) caster sugar, plus about 2 tablespoons caster sugar for sprinkling
100 ml (3½ fl oz) cold water

Spiralizing lemon peel is so much quicker than using a knife to cut strips of peel and results in much prettier spirals. Use this candied peel to decorate cakes such as the Courgette and Lemon Drizzle Cake on page 122.

Cut the lemons in half widthways and squeeze out the juice. (The juice isn't needed for this recipe so store it in the refrigerator to be used another time.) Secure the uncut end of one of the lemon halves to a spiralizer fitted with a ribbon blade and spiralize into strips. Repeat with the remaining lemon halves. Remove any of the pith that has separated from the lemon peel.

Place the caster sugar and measurement water in a small saucepan and bring to the boil, stirring continuously. Add the spiralized lemon peel and boil for 4–5 minutes or until syrupy and the peel is translucent.

Line a baking sheet with nonstick baking paper. Spread out the peel in a single layer on the prepared baking sheet and separate the lemon peel spirals with a fork. Sprinkle over the remaining sugar and then roll the peel in the sugar to coat thoroughly.

Leave the peel to dry in a warm place for a couple of hours, or overnight if possible. The candied peel can be stored for up to 3 weeks in an airtight container.

gooey chocolate and pear puddings

Serves 4
Prepare in 10 minutes
Cook in 20 minutes

2 small firm pears, pointy ends trimmed
150 g (5 oz) butter, softened, plus extra for greasing
200 g (7 oz) soft brown sugar
1 teaspoon vanilla extract
50 g (2 oz) cocoa powder, sifted
125 g (4 oz) self-raising flour, sifted
2 eggs
double cream or crème fraîche, to serve

Grease 4 x 150 ml (¼ pint) pudding tins and line the bases with nonstick baking paper. Using a spiralizer fitted with a 3 mm (⅛ inch) spaghetti blade, spiralize the pears.

Place the butter, sugar and vanilla extract in a large bowl and beat until light and fluffy. Add the cocoa powder, flour and eggs and whisk until combined. Stir in the spiralized pears.

Divide the mixture between the prepared pudding tins. Place the tins on a baking sheet and bake in a preheated oven, 180°C (350°F), Gas Mark 4, for 20 minutes, or until just cooked but still slightly soft in the middle.

Turn out the puddings, remove the baking paper and serve immediately with double cream or crème fraîche.

index

almonds
apple frangipane tart 106
apple, raspberry and almond crumbles 116
apples 6
apple, chicory and walnut salad 44
apple, cinnamon and sultana muffins 119
apple frangipane tart 106
apple, raspberry and almond crumbles 116
baked apple and cinnamon crisps 18
Bramley apple and Calvados sauce 94
pork, apple and sage patties 76
stem ginger and apple cookies 112
Asian coleslaw, spicy 87
Asian pear fruit salad 109
autumn fruit salad 113
autumn minestrone soup 27

bacon
herby sausage and bacon hash 73
Jerusalem artichoke and bacon salad 40
balsamic glaze, roasted beetroot with 100
bean burgers, Mexican spicy 78
beef
beef and broccoli stir-fry 81
cottage pie with crispy topping 54
Thai beef salad 38
beetroot 6
baked vegetable crisps 30
beetroot and blueberry pancakes 118
beetroot and chocolate brownies 108
beetroot, potato and chive rosti 93
beetroot, smoked trout and horseradish salad 49
roasted beetroot with balsamic glaze 100
bhajis, crispy onion 24
blueberries: beetroot and blueberry pancakes 118
borlotti beans: autumn minestrone soup 27
bread: courgette and haloumi bruschetta 17
broccoli 6
beef and broccoli stir-fry 81
brownies, beetroot and chocolate 108
bruschetta, courgette and haloumi 17
burgers
Mexican spicy bean burgers 78
Moroccan turkey burgers 70
butternut squash 6
butternut squash, feta and Puy lentil salad 37
butternut squash, sage and goats' cheese tart 52
butternut squash with ricotta and herbs 69
butternut squash with sage and pine nuts 59
squash, cheese and chive muffins 29

cakes
beetroot and chocolate brownies 108
carrot cake muffins 110
courgette and lemon drizzle cake 122
Calvados: Bramley apple and Calvados sauce 94
candied lemon peel 124
caramel: salted caramel and pear pudding 121
carrots 6
carrot cake muffins 110
cottage pie with crispy topping 54
mooli, carrot and cucumber laksa 16
Moroccan carrot salad 98
Thai beef salad 38
celeriac 6–7
autumn minestrone soup 27
celeriac remoulade 96
mustardy celeriac and potato gratin 90
cheese
butternut squash, feta and Puy lentil salad 37
butternut squash, sage and goats' cheese tart 52
butternut squash with ricotta and herbs 69
courgette and haloumi bruschetta 17
courgette-crust Margherita pizza 77
courgette, feta and mint fritters 13
crispy Parmesan and onion spirals 103
easy potato moussaka 66
Greek salad pitta pockets 19
pear, ham and blue cheese salad 47
pumpkin, cheese and chive muffins 29
see also ricotta cheese
chicken
chicken, courgette and quinoa salad 34
chicken traybake with sweet potatoes 56
green papaya and chicken salad 45
plantain, chicken and coconut curry 74
Vietnamese chicken and noodle salad 46
chicory: apple, chicory and walnut salad 44
chillies: courgetti with crab, chilli and lemon 55
chips: crispy potato fries with rosemary and garlic 91
chives: beetroot, potato and chive rosti 93
chocolate
beetroot and chocolate brownies 108
gooey chocolate and pear puddings 125
chorizo
Mexican baked potato nests 14
Spanish chorizo tortilla 63
chowder, smoked haddock 28
coconut cream: curried sweet potato puffs 58
coconut milk: plantain, chicken and coconut curry 74
cod: spicy baked cod with potato topping 67
coleslaw, spicy Asian 86
cookies, stem ginger and apple 112
cottage pie with crispy topping 54
courgettes 7
chicken, courgette and quinoa salad 34
courgette and haloumi bruschetta 17
courgette and lemon drizzle cake 122
courgette-crust Margherita pizza 77
courgette, feta and mint fritters 13
courgetti with crab, chilli and lemon 55
courgetti with sundried tomato pesto 72
crab
courgetti with crab, chilli and lemon 55
crab and vegetable dim sum 23
crisps
baked apple and cinnamon crisps 18
baked vegetable crisps 30
salt and vinegar baked potato crisps 22
crumble, apple, raspberry and almond 116
cucumber 7
cucumber and mint raita 92
Greek salad pitta pockets 19
mooli, carrot and cucumber laksa 16
spicy cucumber pickle 97
curry
curried sweet potato puffs 58
plantain, chicken and coconut curry 74

daikon radish 7
Japanese tuna tataki salad 36
dauphinoise, sweet potato 86
dill: smoked salmon salad with dill and lemon 41
dim sum, crab and vegetable 23
dip, sumac yogurt 70

edamame beans: vegetable noodle miso soup 10
eggs
Mexican baked potato nests 14

mini sweet potato and ricotta frittatas 20
prawn pad Thai 60
smoked mackerel with quails' egg salad 42
Spanish chorizo tortilla 63

fish
beetroot, smoked trout and horseradish salad 49
Japanese tuna tataki salad 36
sesame and ginger salmon en papilotte 64
smoked haddock chowder 28
smoked haddock fishcakes 82
smoked mackerel with quails' egg salad 42
smoked salmon salad with dill and lemon 41
spicy baked cod with potato topping 67
frangipane: apple frangipane tart 106
fries: crispy potato fries with rosemary and garlic 91
frittatas, mini sweet potato and ricotta 20
fritters
courgette, feta and mint fritters 13
spiced swede and pea fritters 102
fruit
Asian pear fruit salad 109
autumn fruit salad 113
which fruit to spiralize 6–7
see also apples; pears, etc

garlic, crispy potato fries with rosemary and 91
ginger
sesame and ginger salmon en papilotte 64
stem ginger and apple cookies 112
goats' cheese: butternut squash, sage and goats' cheese tart 52
gooey chocolate and pear puddings 125
gratin, mustardy celeriac and potato 90
Greek salad pitta pockets 19
green papaya 7
green papaya and chicken salad 45

haddock
smoked haddock chowder 28
smoked haddock fishcakes 82
haloumi: courgette and haloumi bruschetta 17
ham: pear, ham and blue cheese salad 47
herbs
butternut squash with ricotta and herbs 69
herby sausage and bacon hash 73
honey, steamed vegetables with 101
horseradish: beetroot, smoked trout and horseradish salad 49

Japanese tuna tataki salad 36
Jerusalem artichokes 7
Jerusalem artichoke and bacon salad 40

laksa, mooli, carrot and cucumber 16
lamb: easy potato moussaka 66
lemons
candied lemon peel 124
courgette and lemon drizzle cake 122
courgetti with crab, chilli and lemon 55
smoked salmon salad with dill and lemon 41
lentils: butternut squash, feta and Puy lentil salad 37

mackerel: smoked mackerel with quails' egg salad 42
mayonnaise: celeriac remoulade 96
Mexican baked potato nests 14
Mexican spicy bean burgers 78
minestrone soup, autumn 27
mint
courgette, feta and mint fritters 13
cucumber and mint raita 92
miso soup, vegetable noodle 10
mooli 7
mooli, carrot and cucumber laksa 16
prawn pad Thai 60
prawn rice paper wraps 12
spicy Asian coleslaw 86
Thai beef salad 38
Moroccan carrot salad 98
Moroccan turkey burgers 70
moussaka, easy potato 66
muffins
apple, cinnamon and sultana muffins 119
carrot cake muffins 110
pumpkin, cheese and chive muffins 29
mustardy celeriac and potato gratin 90

noodles
beef and broccoli stir-fry 81
Vietnamese chicken and noodle salad 46

oats: stem ginger and apple cookies 112
olives: Greek salad pitta pockets 19
onions 7
crispy onion bhajis 24
crispy Parmesan and onion spirals 103

pad Thai, prawn 60
pancakes, beetroot and blueberry 118
pancetta: autumn minestrone soup 27
parsnips 7
baked vegetable crisps 30
spiralized root vegetable rosti 88
pastry puffs, curried sweet potato 58
patties, pork, apple and sage 76
pears 7
gooey chocolate and pear puddings 125
pear, ham and blue cheese salad 47
pear tarte tatin 114
salted caramel and pear pudding 121
peas
butternut squash with ricotta and herbs 69
spiced swede and pea fritters 102
pesto, sundried tomato 72
pickle, spicy cucumber 97
pine nuts, butternut squash with sage and 59
pitta pockets, Greek salad 19
pizza, courgette-crust Margherita 77
plantains 7
plantain, chicken and coconut curry 74
pomegranate seeds
Asian pear fruit salad 109
chicken, courgette and quinoa salad 34
pork, apple and sage patties 76
potatoes 7
beetroot, potato and chive rosti 93
crispy potato fries with rosemary and garlic 91
crispy potato straws 42
easy potato moussaka 66
herby sausage and bacon hash 73
Mexican baked potato nests 14
mustardy celeriac and potato gratin 90
salt and vinegar baked potato crisps 22
smoked haddock chowder 28
smoked haddock fishcakes 82
Spanish chorizo tortilla 63
spicy baked cod with potato topping 67
spicy potato curls 95
spiralized root vegetable rosti 88
sweet potato dauphinoise 86
prawns
prawn pad Thai 60
prawn rice paper wraps 12
pumpkin, cheese and chive muffins 29

quails' eggs: smoked mackerel with quails' egg salad 42
quinoa: chicken, courgette and quinoa salad 34

raita, cucumber and mint 92
raspberries: apple, raspberry and almond crumbles 116
red kidney beans: Mexican spicy bean burgers 78
remoulade, celeriac 96
rice noodles: Vietnamese chicken and noodle salad 46
rice paper wraps, prawn 12
ricotta cheese
butternut squash with ricotta and herbs 69
mini sweet potato and ricotta frittatas 20
rosemary: crispy potato fries with rosemary and garlic 91
rosti
beetroot, potato and chive rosti 93
spiralized root vegetable rosti 88

sage
butternut squash, sage and goats' cheese tart 52
butternut squash with sage and pine nuts 59
pork, apple and sage patties 76
salads 32–49
apple, chicory and walnut salad 44
Asian pear fruit salad 109
autumn fruit salad 113
beetroot, smoked trout and horseradish salad 49
butternut squash, feta and Puy lentil salad 37
chicken, courgette and quinoa salad 34
Greek salad pitta pockets 19
green papaya and chicken salad 45
Japanese tuna tataki salad 36
Jerusalem artichoke and bacon salad 40
Moroccan carrot salad 98
pear, ham and blue cheese salad 47
smoked mackerel with quails' egg salad 42
smoked salmon salad with dill and lemon 41
spicy Asian coleslaw 86
Thai beef salad 38
Vietnamese chicken and noodle salad 46
salmon
sesame and ginger salmon en papilotte 64
smoked salmon salad with dill and lemon 41
salt and vinegar baked potato crisps 22
salted caramel and pear pudding 121
sauce, Bramley apple and Calvados 94
sausages: herby sausage and bacon hash 73
sesame and ginger salmon en papilotte 64
smoked haddock
smoked haddock chowder 28
smoked haddock fishcakes 82
smoked mackerel with quails' egg salad 42
smoked salmon salad with dill and lemon 41
smoked trout: beetroot, smoked trout and horseradish salad 49
soups
autumn minestrone soup 27
mooli, carrot and cucumber laksa 16
Spanish chorizo tortilla 63
spinach
butternut squash with ricotta and herbs 69
plantain, chicken and coconut curry 74
spicy baked cod with potato topping 67
spiral vegetable tempura 26
spiralized root vegetable rosti 88
spiralizers, introduction to 4–6
stir-fry, beef and broccoli 81
storing spiralized vegetables 7
sultanas: apple, cinnamon and sultana muffins 119
sumac yogurt dip 70
sundried tomato pesto 72
swede 7
spiced swede and pea fritters 102
sweet potatoes 7
baked vegetable crisps 30
chicken traybake with sweet potatoes 56
curried sweet potato puffs 58
Mexican spicy bean burgers 78
mini sweet potato and ricotta frittatas 20
sweet potato dauphinoise 86

tarts
apple frangipane tart 106
butternut squash, sage and goats' cheese tart 52
pear tarte tatin 114
tempura, spiral vegetable 26
Thai beef salad 38
tomatoes
courgette-crust Margherita pizza 77
easy potato moussaka 66
Greek salad pitta pockets 19
sundried tomato pesto 72
tortilla, Spanish chorizo 63
trout: beetroot, smoked trout and horseradish salad 49
tuna: Japanese tuna tataki salad 36
turkey burgers, Moroccan 70

vegetables
baked vegetable crisps 30
cooking and storing 7
crab and vegetable dim sum 23
spiral vegetable tempura 26
spiralized root vegetable rosti 88
steamed vegetables with honey 101
vegetable noodle miso soup 10
which vegetables to use 6–7
see also carrots; potatoes, etc
Vietnamese chicken and noodle salad 46

walnuts: apple, chicory and walnut salad 44

yogurt
cucumber and mint raita 92
easy potato moussaka 66
sumac yogurt dip 70

acknowledgements

Thank you to UK Juicers (**www.ukjuicers.com**) for loaning us the spiralizers for the photoshoot.

Senior Commissioning Editor: Eleanor Maxfield
Project Editor: Clare Churly
Art Director: Tracy Killick at Tracy Killick Art Direction and Design
Photographer: William Shaw
Food Stylist: Denise Smart
Prop Stylist: Kim Sullivan
Assistant Production Manager: Caroline Alberti